Museums in the Landscape:
Bridging the Gap

Society of Museum Archaeologists
The Museum Archaeologist
Volume 23
Conference Proceedings
St Albans 1996

Edited by: G T Denford
Society of Museum Archaeologists

Society of Museum Archaeologists

ISBN 1 871855 11 X

Printed in Great Britain
Published by the Society of Museum Archaeologists
c/o G.T. Denford
Hon. Editor, SMA
Historic Resources Centre
75 Hyde Street
Winchester
SO23 7DW

FOREWORD

This volume of *The Museum Archaeologist* contains the majority of the papers given at the annual conference of the Society held in St Albans in November 1996.

The conference programme has been included and follows the Preface written by the conference organiser, Vivienne Holgate. The papers are arranged in the order in which they were delivered at the conference.

The paper presented by Paul Miles has herein been contributed by Ian George. Nick Merriman and John Marjoram requested that their papers should not be included in the publication. The presentation by Mark Davies *An Archaeological Park in the Making at Gosbecks Farm, Colchester* will be incorporated in the next issue of *The Museum Archaeologist*, volume 24, with updated information.

Finally, a comment by Mark Hall has been added, teasing out, in his view, the two underlying threads of the conference.

G.T. Denford
Hon. Editor
December 1997

Front cover illustration:
Interior view of the new entrance area, Verulamium Museum, St Albans

CONTENTS

PREFACE

The 1996 SMA Conference was held at Verulamium Museum, St Albans. As the site museum at the centre of Roman Verulamium, this was an appropriate choice of venue in view of the conference title and subject matter.

Several papers reflected the increasing use of information technology in archaeology today as a means of 'bridging the gap' between curated remains and access to them. Case studies were presented relating to museum displays, the transfer of information onto the internet, electronic publishing and Urban Archaeological Database projects. The UADs, which were intended priamarily for developing planning-related archaeological strategies, have proved to be extremely useful research tools and must encourage museum-based curators to look beyond their own collection databases and consider how they can be used in conjunction with electronic mapping and landscape-centred systems.

The central theme of the conference was the preservation, display and recording of archaeological remains in the landscape and their associated archives. Four 'museums in the landscape' were examined. These dated from the Roman period through to an eighteenth century industrial landscape and twentieth century military defences. Each looked at a variety of issues, including fieldwork, reseach, conservation, management, interpretation, promotion and outreach.

Other papers addressed a number of highly topical issues. These ranged from the storage of archives to copyright and the use of archives for research. In addition, an overview was presented of the progress of the Treasure Bill, the voluntary Code of Practice and the proposed pilot recording projects. By the time this is in print, the Treasure Act will be in force and a survey on the transfer of archives to museums will have been commissioned by English Heritage and the Museums and Galleries Commission.

The conference finished with a tour of archaeological sites in the county. These included the excavations taking place prior to the building of the new extension at Verulamium Museum, Welwyn Roman Baths, and the *oppidum* at Devil's Dyke, Wheathampstead.

On behalf of SMA I would like to thank St Albans District Council for their hospitality and all those members of staff at both Verulamium Museum and the Museum of St Albans who were involved in organising the conference. Thanks also to Welwyn Hatfield Museum Service, and to Hartley McMaster Ltd and Hertfordshire County Council Archaeology Section for their IT demonstrations.

Vivienne Holgate, Verulamium Museum
Conference Organiser

THURSDAY 14 NOVEMBER

1930 Welcome: *The Right Worshipful Mayor of St Albans, Reverend Councillor Robert Donald*

Keynote address: **Current Developments on Treasure and Portable Antiquities**
Roger Bland (British Museum/Department of National Heritage)

Reception

FRIDAY 15 NOVEMBER
Session 1: **Archaeology and Information Technology**
Chair: *Robin Boast (University Museum of Archaeology and Anthropology, Cambridge)*

0930-1000 **An Urban Archaeological Database for St Albans**
Isobel Thompson (St Albans District Council)
1000-1030 **Winchester Urban Archaeological Database: the next step**
Richard Whinney (Winchester Museums Service)

1030-1100 Coffee

1100-1130 **The Lincoln Urban Archaeological Database**
Paul Miles (City of Lincoln Archaeology Unit)
1130-1200 **Deposit Modelling in the Urban Archaeological Database in Plymouth**
Keith Ray and Sarah Noble (Plymouth City Council)
1200-1230 **Electronic Journals and Archiving**
Alan Vince (University of York)
1230-1245 Discussion

1245-1400 Lunch

Session 2: **Museums in the Landscape**
Chair: *David Allen (Andover Museum, Hampshire County Museum Service)*

1400-1430 **An Archaeological Park in the Making at Gosbecks Farm, Colchester**
Mark Davies (Colchester Museums)
1430-1500 **Caistor St Edmund and Burgh Castle: Recent Work of the Norfolk Archaeological Trust**
John Davies (Castle Museum, Norwich)
1500-1530 **A Welsh Perspective: Interpreting the Industrial History of Minerva and Bersham**
John Marjoram (Wrexham County Museum)

1530-1600 Tea

1600-1630 **CBA Defence of Britain Project**
Jim Earle (Council for British Archaeology)
1630-1700 **IT in Museum Displays: The Next n Years**
Edmund Southworth (Liverpool Museum, National Museums and Galleries on Merseyside)
1700-1715 Discussion

1900 for 1930 Welcome: *Peter Lerner (Director of Planning and Heritage, St Albans District Council)*

Buffet, and an opportunity to surf the archaeological Internet and view the Hertfordshire SMR GIS application

SATURDAY 16 NOVEMBER
Session 3: **Archives and Access: Some Regional and National Studies**
Chair: *Janet Owen (Department of Museum Studies, Leicester University)*

0930-1000 **SPECTRUM: A Ray of Light for Archaeologists**
Christine Longworth (Liverpool Museum, National Museums and Galleries on Merseyside)
1000-1030 **Copyright and Access**
Neil Beagrie (RCHME)

1030-1100 Coffee

1100-1130 **Case Study: Surrey Archaeological Museum Survey**
Hedley Swain (Museum of London Archaeology Service)
1130-1200 **Problems and Practicalities in Archive-based Research**
Jo Brück (University of Cambridge)
1200-1230 **A Crisis in Archaeological Archives? Discussion**
Nick Merriman (Museum of London)

1230-1345 Lunch

Afternoon Session: Site Visits
1345-dusk Tour of the current excavation at Roman Verulamium, Welwyn Roman Baths, and the Oppidum at Wheathampstead

2

THE TREASURE ACT AND THE PROPOSALS FOR THE VOLUNTARY RECORDING OF ALL ARCHAEOLOGICAL FINDS

Roger Bland, British Museum/Department of National Heritage

In July 1996 the Treasure Act, the first law governing portable antiquities ever passed in England and Wales, achieved Royal Assent. This law will come into force on 24 September 1997, following Parliamentary approval for the Code of Practice in March 1997. At the same time five Government-funded pilot schemes for the voluntary recording of all archaeological finds will commence in Kent, Norfolk, York, Liverpool and Scunthorpe (in addition the British Museum will be funding a sixth post in the West Midlands). This paper sets out the background to the new law, describes its main points and discusses the initiative for the recording of all archaeological finds. It is based on a paper given to the Society of Museum Archaeologists' conference in November 1996, but was revised in July 1997 to take account of developments since then, principally the drafting of the Code of Practice on the Treasure Act and the announcement regarding pilot schemes. This is an area where matters are developing quickly and a further progress report will appear in the SMA Newsletter.

Treasure trove

Treasure trove was Germanic in origin and its adoption in England probably goes back to Anglo-Saxon times (Hill 1936; Palmer 1993; Bland 1996). The essence of the Germanic principle of treasure trove was that all treasure should belong to the King and there was a fundamental contrast with the Latin system where treasure belonged equally to finder and landowner. English treasure trove law first became formulated in the 12th and 13th centuries AD: and until this year it had hardly changed since the account of Henry de Bracton (*De legibus et consuetudinibus Angliae*) written in about 1250. Because it was common law, there was no definitive written account of treasure trove. However, the basic principles of treasure trove are well-known: all gold and silver objects had to be reported to coroner who would hold an inquest to decide whether they would be treasure trove. In order to be treasure trove an object had to pass three tests: it had to be made of gold or silver; it had to have been buried with the intention of recovery; and its original owner or his heirs must be unknown. If a find was treasure trove then in law it became Crown property, but since 1886 the Crown has paid rewards for those objects which museums wish to retain or else it has returned the find. One problem with the law of treasure trove was the very big gap between the reporting requirement - all gold and silver objects - and those which were actually declared to be treasure trove, which only amounted to a small proportion of all gold and silver objects. Under the Treasure Act only those objects which are treasure need to be reported.

In recent years twenty to thirty finds a year were declared treasure trove (see the *Annual Reports of the Treasure Trove Reviewing Committee*); ninety per cent of them were coin hoards, the others being finds of gold and silver jewellery and plate. Ninety per cent of treasure troves were found with metal detectors, the remainder being chance discoveries found during building or earth-moving works, or in the course of archaeological excavations.

Since the middle of the last century it was appreciated that treasure trove did not provide a significant addition to the Crown's revenues since there was no incentive for finders to report their finds and the practice arose of paying rewards to the finder. This was the result of many years of pressure from interested reformers, especially Lord Talbot de Malahide, who had introduced a Private Member's Bill to reform treasure trove in 1858 (it failed) (Carman 1996). Finally, in 1886, the Treasury issued a minute stating that objects that had been declared treasure trove should be sent to the British Museum for valuation; that the British Museum should have the right to acquire any objects that they wanted and that they should then be offered to other museums (usually the local museum); and that the finder should receive an *ex gratia* reward, provided he had behaved properly. At first the Treasury knocked a percentage off the reward to cover administrative costs, but in 1931, after a campaign by George Hill of the British Museum, the Treasury was persuaded to pay the full amount to the finder. This remains the current basis for the administration of treasure trove, with the National Museum of Wales (now the National Museums & Galleries of Wales) taking over the British Museum's functions in respect of finds in Wales in the 1940s.

One result of this concession was that the Treasury decided that the museum which wishes to acquire the find has to find the money to pay the reward out of its own resources and as a consequence many finds are not acquired because of the difficulty museums have in raising the money.

Problems of treasure trove
Since treasure trove only included objects that contained a substantial proportion of gold or silver it afforded no protection at all to the great majority of archaeological finds, even though they might have been of great historical or cultural value. Despite Lord Denning's judgement of 1981 (1 All E R 524) that objects had to contain 'substantial' amounts of gold or silver in order to qualify as treasure trove, each find that occurred since then was dealt with differently. One example was the group of torcs, bracelets and ingots discovered at Snettisham in Norfolk in 1990. These have been described as 'by far the greatest concentration of buried wealth from any British early Iron Age context' (Stead 1991; Longworth 1992), and yet because some of the objects contained fifty per cent or more of base metal, only those objects of a higher purity were declared treasure trove.

Hoards of Roman coins of the mid- 3rd century AD, which are very common in Britain, posed a particular problem under the treasure trove system. This is because they typically contain coins made over a period of up to a hundred years which consist of ever-decreasing amounts of silver. Since Lord Denning's judgement coroners' inquests took widely differing views on how to deal with coin hoards of this period. Several hoards containing gold and silver objects of varying degrees of fineness were split into portions that were declared treasure trove and portions that were not (for details see Bland 1996, 17, n 26).

Even more serious perhaps was the fact that many entire hoards of Roman coins were not considered as treasure trove because they were made of very base silver or bronze and, since there was no requirement to report them, many were perfectly legally sold and dispersed before they could be recorded. Thus the information they contained was lost for ever. A good example was the hoard of 47,912 base silver coins of the 3rd century AD discovered at Normanby in Lincolnshire in 1985 (Bland and Burnett 1988). This was the second largest hoard of coins ever to have been found in this country and several members of staff at the British Museum spent over a year cleaning and studying it. At an inquest at Lincoln in May 1987 it was declared not to be treasure

trove on the grounds that the silver content of the coins was too low and the whole hoard was sold the next day to a dealer. As a result the British Museum was unable to acquire many of the coins from the hoard that it wished to add to its collection. This was a particular loss as the study of the Normanby hoard has formed the basis of our understanding of the coinage of this period.

In fact, however, the Normanby hoard was only the largest of a series of more than twenty major coin hoards of this period which were found in the last fifteen years and which were not treasure trove. In 1993 alone, twenty-one new Roman coin hoards were reported; twelve were not treasure trove and several were broken up before any record could be made. A case in point was a hoard of about 1,500 bronze coins of the late 4th century AD from Amersham in Buckinghamshire. This hoard was found in 1986 but was perfectly legally dispersed shortly afterwards and it only came to light subsequently because the finder's mother wrote an account of its discovery in the magazine *Take a Break* (15 January 1994). No full record of it will ever be made (Bland and Orna-Ornstein 1997). Under the Treasure Act all hoards of coins that are at least 300 years old are treasure (see below).

In addition to the requirement that an object should be made substantially of gold or silver, it was also necessary to establish that its original owner concealed it with the intention of recovering it later, and did not simply lose or abandon it. It was absurd to think that we could understand the motives that led their owners to bury objects such as gold torcs several thousand years ago and yet this was a question that regularly arose at treasure inquests. In any case this was a completely irrelevant consideration when deciding whether antiquities should be preserved for the nation. Thus, for example, the Bronze Age gold torc found at Monkton Deverill in Wiltshire in 1991 was the subject of a long and costly process of litigation in order to decide this very point (Ward 1994). The Treasure Act removes the need to determine the motives of the original owners of such objects, since all objects other than coins that have a precious metal content of at least 10% and that are at least 300 years old are treasure, however they came to be placed in the ground (see below).

What is more, single objects, however important they might have been, were seldom declared treasure trove because it was generally considered that they were more likely to have been lost than deliberately buried. A well-known example was the Middleham jewel, discovered in Yorkshire in 1985, and described as "the most important piece of medieval jewellery discovered in

England in this century" (Cherry 1994). It was not treasure trove since it could not be shown to have been deliberately buried with the intention of recovery. It was sold at auction in 1986 for £1,300,000 and in 1990 the purchaser applied for an export licence, a valuation of £2,500,000 being placed it. The export licence was deferred in order to allow a British institution time to raise the money required and after an appeal it was acquired by the Yorkshire Museum. Under the Treasure Act protection is provided to single precious metal objects such as the Middleham jewel.

In the same way, objects buried in graves did not qualify as treasure trove, since they too could not be said to have been buried with the intention of recovery. Thus the Sutton Hoo ship burial was not treasure trove for this reason, and it was only possible for the British Museum to acquire this unique find for the nation through the generosity of the landowner, Mrs Pretty (Hill 1975). Precious metal objects from graves, together with any associated finds, also receive protection under the Treasure Act (see below).

Another anomaly of the old system was that objects which were made of base metal, or of some other material, received no legal protection at all, even if they were found in association with objects that were treasure trove. Thus the pots in which coin hoards were found were not declared treasure trove, even though they might have been of considerable archaeological importance. Similarly, the very fine shale box which accompanied the hoard of late Roman gold and silver from Thetford was not treasure trove (Johns and Potter 1983), nor were the engraved gems from the Roman jeweller's hoard found at Snettisham (Johns 1997). This was discovered in 1986 and consisted of 89 silver finger-rings, bracelets, pendants and chains and silver bars; 110 unmounted cornelian gems (and another 17 set in finger-rings); 83 silver and 27 bronze coins of the 1st and 2nd centuries AD and a pot. The hoard was declared treasure trove with the exception of the gems, bronze coins and pot which were excluded because they were not made of precious metal. Under the Treasure Act objects found in clear archaeological association with objects that are treasure are also protected (see below).

So the old law needed reform because it was riddled with anomalies and not because there was a need to clamp down on metal detecting. There is no doubt, however, that the great increase in finds that has resulted from the widespread use of metal detectors has highlighted the problem.

The Treasure Act is a very modest reform. A recent survey by the CBA suggested that perhaps 400,000 archaeological objects are being found each year with metal detectors (Dobinson and Denison 1995). Over the last ten years on average twenty-two finds a year have been declared treasure trove. These twenty-two finds comprise on average 7,500 individual objects, so these amount to less than two per cent of the total number of objects being found. We believe that the Act may double the number of cases of treasure, but of course this would only increase the proportion from two per cent to four per cent of all objects found.

Other countries
One of the curiosities of treasure trove is that the English law does not apply to the whole of the United Kingdom. In Scotland all newly discovered archaeological objects, whether they are of precious metal or not and regardless of whether they were hidden or lost, belong to the Crown under the legal principle of *bona vacantia* (Sheridan 1991; Sheridan 1994; Sheridan 1995; Carey Miller and Sheridan 1997). Although the Crown only chooses to exercise its claim in certain cases, this does mean that in Scotland all archaeological objects must be reported and the Crown can claim those which it believes to be sufficiently important. Northern Ireland, on the other hand, has the same treasure trove law as England and Wales, and so it is included within the scope of the Act, but there is also a statutory duty to report all archaeological objects in the Province. The Northern Irish law also states that a licence is needed to search for archaeological objects with a metal detector (Historic Monuments and Archaeological Objects (Northern Ireland) Order 1995 sections 29, 41 and 42).

In the Republic of Ireland, the National Monuments (Amendment) Act 1994 makes all archaeological objects discovered in the Republic the property of the state. It is an offence to own or trade in archaeological objects from the soil of the Republic and the law contains retrospective provisions requiring all privately owned antiquities found in the Republic since the passage of the first National Monuments Act in 1930 to be reported within three months of the enactment of the law. Metal detecting is outlawed and metal detecting magazines are banned. These measures seem draconian to anyone brought up in the English tradition of respect for private property, but they enjoy widespread support in the Republic where it is thought to be entirely right that the nations's archaeological heritage should be protected in this way (Anon 1994; Kelly 1995).

In fact a survey of legislation in twenty-one other European countries shows that the legal protection afforded portable antiquities in England and Wales is at the same time more limited in scope and more permissive and also more liberal in its treatment of finders than in virtually any other country in Europe (see Appendix). Thus only Belgium has a weaker legal requirement to report finds and provides legal protection to a smaller range of objects than England and Wales. As regards the use of metal detectors, in most countries all archaeological excavation is controlled and metal detectors can only be used under licence and these are not normally given to treasure hunters (the only exceptions being some of the Scandinavian countries). We have no controls on the use of metal detectors in this country - except on scheduled sites - and the Treasure Act contains no restrictions on their use. Lastly, as regards rewards, the practice in England and Wales of paying the finder the full market value as assessed by an independent committee, is more liberal than most countries, in many of which the reward bears little relation to the market value. In fact all these countries have passed laws to protect their heritage of movable archaeological objects this century. They see this as a completely natural thing to do and when viewed against this background, one can see that the Treasure Act will only make a very modest change to our current law.

The history of attempts at reform

After Lord Talbot's Bill of 1858 and Sir George Hill's efforts in the 1930s to ensure that full rewards were paid, the movement for reform started in earnest again after the Second World War. In 1944 one of the aims of the newly established Council for British Archaeology was to reform the law of treasure trove and in the 1970s the Council for British Archaeology sponsored a Bill to reform the law which was introduced into the Lords by Lord Abinger in 1979 and again in 1982 (Cleere 1991 and 1994). However, it did not have Government support - mainly because landowning interests opposed it - and it failed in the Commons (Bland 1996, 21).

Towards the end of the 1980s, the Surrey Archaeological Society began to plan a new Bill, spurred on by the looting of Wanborough where several individuals were caught removing Iron Age coins illegally from the site, but the subsequent prosecutions failed because of the anomalies of the law of treasure trove (O'Connell and Bird 1994). The Surrey Society worked closely with the British Museum and enlisted the tireless support of Lord Perth and the Bill was drafted after extensive consultation. In 1992 the Department of National Heritage was created and a year later it took over responsibility for

treasure trove from the Treasury and so for the first time Government policy on archaeological and portable antiquities was all dealt with in one place. In March 1994 Lord Perth introduced the Treasure Bill as a Private Member's Bill in the House of Lords. The Bill had general support in the Lords - including Government support - but it failed in the Commons where it did not receive any time for debate and was the subject of political skulduggery (for the references to the debates see Bland 1996, 24). In November 1995, Sir Anthony Grant MP, who gained a place in the ballot for Private Member's Bills announced that he was going to take on the Bill. On this occasion there was ample time for debate - it was debated for more than six hours altogether - and it passed through both Houses with all-party support and without opposition. It received Royal Assent on 4 July (Commons, 2nd Reading, 8 March 1996; Standing Committee F, 17 April; 3rd Reading, 10 May; Lords, 2nd Reading, 5 June; Committee, 19 June; 3rd Reading, 26 June).

The Code of Practice

The passage of the Treasure Act only marked the first stage of the process needed before it could actually come into force. The Act contained a provision requiring a Code of Practice to be drawn up in consultation with interested parties and this code, together with any revision of it, had to be approved by Parliament under the 'affirmative resolution' procedure, meaning that it had to be debated in both Houses. The Act states that the Code should set out the guidelines to be followed by the Secretary of State in the payment of rewards and in deciding whether to disclaim a find and that it may also provide guidance to finders and others concerned with treasure. A separate Code has been drawn up for Northern Ireland to take account of the different legislative régime that exists in the Province (see above), although in all other respects it follows exactly the same policy as the version drawn up for England and Wales.

The first draft of the Code of Practice was issued for consultation on 17 December with a request for comments by 14 February. Some 1,500 copies were sent out and all the main interested parties - including metal detecting clubs, leading archaeological societies and museums bodies, selected museums, antiquities and coin dealers and landowners' groups - were given an opportunity to comment. The Department received over 250 responses, most of which came from metal detectorists, and the Code of Practice was substantially revised to take account of their concerns and of the comments received from archaeologists and museums. There is no doubt that the revised draft represents a substantial improvement on the first draft. It provides greater clarity on many points which were not spelled out as fully as they might have been in the first draft. It lays greater emphasis on the role of local government archaeologists and local museums, proposing that local arrangements for the reporting and delivery of finds should be drawn up for each of the 139 coroners' districts in England and Wales.

The revised draft was then circulated to the fifty or so organisations most closely interested in it. Further comments were received from twenty or so organisations and these were incorporated into the final draft (thus, for example, all four suggestions made by the National Council for Metal Detecting were incorporated into the final draft). The Code was approved by both Houses after short debates (Commons, 18 March 1997 and Lords, 20 March 1997) and the Act will come into force on 24 September 1997.

The Code of Practice is to be distributed in August 1997 together with a leaflet summarising the main points. The Department is distributing both documents as widely as possible, printing 22,000 copies of the former and 85,000 copies of the latter. They provide a very important tool for educating the public, especially metal detectorists, about the Act and about good practice in general. The publicity campaign involved in distributing the Code and informing detectorists, museums, archaeologists and coroners about the new arrangements will be an opportunity to stress the message of the importance of the reporting of finds.

Opposition to the Bill: metal detectorists

I want now to look briefly at the opposition that the Bill faced during its long period of gestation, because it is the nature of the opposition that actually explains why the Act looks like it does. The one major body to oppose the Bill was the National Council for Metal Detecting. This, it seems, is not so much because the Act contains anything harmful to their interests - it does not - but because of a long history of distrust between archaeologists and metal detectorists. This probably was not helped by the fact that the Act was originally an initiative of the Surrey Archaeological Society who started it as a response to the looting of the site at Wanborough (see above).

The Department of National Heritage have had a number of discussions with representatives of the National Council for Metal Detecting and in the spring of 1995 they produced a considered response outlining their objections to the Bill. As a result the Bill's sponsors

made five amendments to meet their concerns, a fairly substantial package. The changes were as follows: (a) the minimum precious metal needed for objects to be treasure was raised from 5% to 10%; (b) the minimum number of base-metal coins that would be treasure if they are from the same find was raised from 2 to 10; (c) the Secretary of State was given the power to disclaim objects that have been submitted as treasure; (d) coroners were given discretion as to whether to summon juries to treasure inquests (previously all treasure inquests were to be held without a jury) and (e) coroners are required to inform the finder if they intend to hold a treasure inquest and to give them the opportunity to examine witnesses. On the other hand none of these changes weakened the archaeological impact of the Bill: they simply made it more workable. In addition, ministers stated during the debates on the Bill in Parliament that the Government had no intention of banning or otherwise restricting responsible metal-detecting, nor is it the first step down a road which would eventually result in compulsory reporting of all finds or the licensing of all detectorists. Some archaeologists might regret that, but the logic of the voluntary pilot schemes is that they will only work if there is trust on both sides, so the Government is fully committed to a voluntary approach.

View that the Bill nationalises private property

Secondly, the view has also been expressed that giving legal protection to additional categories of objects is tantamount to nationalisation by the state and represents an attack on private property rights. This opinion has been expressed very strongly by Andrew Selkirk in *Current Archaeology* (Selkirk 1994a and 1994b) and was shared by at least one MP who objected to the Bill in 1994. In fact, though, the Bill was supported by the two main landowners' organisations - the Country Landowners Association and the National Farmers Union - because in return for widening the scope of treasure in a modest way it gives them two important benefits that they did not previously enjoy. Firstly, it gives them the right to be informed of finds of treasure from their land and, secondly, it makes them eligible for rewards. It is also, of course, the case that even after the new Act has come into force far fewer archaeological objects are subject to legal protection in England and Wales than in other countries of Europe.

View that the Bill does not go far enough

Lastly, at the opposite end of the spectrum, Tim Schadla-Hall has condemned the Bill as an unhappy compromise which is far too limited in its scope, arguing that its enactment will make it harder to secure what they believe is really needed, which is full-scale portable antiquities legislation (Schadla-Hall 1994). A motion to this effect was passed at the conference of the Museums Association in 1994, although it was subsequently repudiated by the Council of the Museums Association (*Museums Journal* October 1994, 46; see also Schadla-Hall 1995a and 1995b and Renfrew 1995). It is undoubtedly true that the Act is a compromise and it is always easy to criticise compromises, but more comprehensive legislation would require substantial new resources and would not obtain Government support. Furthermore, legislation extending state ownership to all archaeological finds would run into very severe opposition not just from 30,000 metal-detectorists, but also from those who object to any extension of state ownership. The Treasure Act was in fact the best that could be achieved within the very tight constraints that have been imposed on it, the main one being that it should have no resource implications. Most archaeologists now take a more pragmatic line and in May 1995 the Council for British Archaeology's Standing Conference on Portable Antiquities, which brings together all leading archaeological and museum organisations, unanimously approved a motion endorsing the Treasure Act (see Bland 1996, 25).

I think it is both interesting and depressing to reflect why the very modest degree of reform embodied in the Treasure Act took so long to achieve in this country. One reason seems to be that England lacks the nationalistic feeling that its archaeological heritage is something that should be preserved that one finds in Scotland and Northern Ireland. But most importantly archaeologists have failed to persuade public opinion that the our archaeological heritage is something worth protecting. I am quite sure that archaeologists have a big job of public education to do. I hope that the effort put into consulting on and then distributing the Code of Practice and also in setting up a recording scheme can go some way in this direction, but the need to convince the public that archaeology is important is obviously something that we all need to bear in mind.

The Treasure Act and Code of Practice
The new provisions only apply to objects found after 24 September, so that detectorists and others who already have collections of finds will not be required to register them.

The new definition of treasure is as follows:

(i) **Objects other than coins**: any object other than a coin provided at least 10 per cent gold or silver and at least 300 years old when found. (The figure was set at 10 per cent to exclude objects with gold or silver plating.)

(ii) **Coins**: all coins from the 'same find' (see below) provided they are at least 300 years old. In case of base metal coins there must be a minimum of ten coins and in case of gold and silver coins a minimum of two. There is a list of coins with less than ten per cent of gold or silver in Appendix 4 of the Code of Practice.

(iii) **Objects found in association with objects that are treasure**: any object, of whatever composition, that is found in the same place as, or that had previously been together with, another object that is treasure.

(iv) **Objects that would have been treasure trove**: any object that would previously have been treasure trove, but does not fall within the specific categories given above. In practice such finds are generally likely to be hoards of coins of the 18th, 19th or 20th centuries and these are very rare, there being only one or two such cases a year. Single coins found on their own are not treasure.

Same find
This is essentially an archaeological concept which proved difficult to deal with in a legal document. The Act states that an object is part of the 'same find' as another object if it is found in the same place as, or had previously been left together with, the other object. The Code notes that it will be for the coroner's inquest to establish these facts and circumstances will vary from case to case, but in general, the definition of the 'same place' should be taken to mean a place of deposition where the objects are found physically together or, if dispersed, may reasonably be supposed to have once been in physical association. Dispersal might, for example, occur through agricultural activity or construction work, through the burrowing of animals, or through other agencies and so the current and previous use of the land where the find has been made will often be a determining factor.

So far as concerns coin finds, the Code makes it clear that only the following three categories will usually be considered to be treasure: (a) hoards, which have been deliberately hidden; (b) groups such as the contents of purses, which may have been dropped or lost and (c) votive or ritual deposits. In the case of votive deposits, the 'same place' may include deposition in a well or sacred spring or within a temple precinct, or within a similar location judged to be of ritual purpose. Assemblages of coins that may reasonably be interpreted as individual losses accumulated over a period of time and that were in all probability never deposited in physical association (for example those found on settlement sites or on fair sites) should not normally be considered treasure. The Code notes that most hoards and purses are not associated with settlement or fair sites, although they may be.

There is also a provision in the Act that allows additional categories of object to be designated as treasure and a parallel one that allows them to be removed from the designation of treasure. This gives the Act great flexibility as it means that it will be possible to adjust the definition in the light of experience and the Code states that the definition of treasure will be looked at in a review that will be carried out after three years.

Objects from wrecks and those found on consecrated land of the Church of England (except for finds that would have qualified as treasure trove) are excluded from the definition of treasure. The Act only includes man-made objects: it excludes, for example, human and animal remains, even if they are found in association with objects that are treasure. It also excludes naturally occurring gold and silver, such as gold nuggets.

The reporting of finds

This is the issue that caused most difficulties in drafting the Code of Practice. The Act only states that (a) all finds have to be reported to the coroner and (b) that the coroner has to inform the British Museum (or the National Museums & Galleries of Wales) if he intends to hold an inquest. All the details of how the initial reporting of finds should work were left to the Code of Practice.

The Act states that a person who finds an object which he believes or has reasonable grounds for believing is treasure must notify the coroner for the district in which the object within fourteen days of making find or within fourteen days of believing the object to be treasure. It is important to stress that the Act requires a finder to report his find and not to deliver it within that period. If a finder discovers an object that he does not immediately believe to be treasure but learns subsequently that it may be treasure, for example, after cleaning it or examining it more closely at a later date, or after having it identified by a museum, then he should report it within fourteen days of realising that it may be treasure. It is a criminal offence, with a maximum penalty of three months im-

prisonment or £5,000 fine or both, not to report a find of treasure to the coroner. It is worth noting that the penalty for not reporting treasure is not new: failure to report treasure trove counted as theft of Crown property.

The Act states that it will be a valid defence if the finder can show that he had a 'reasonable excuse' for failing to notify the coroner. For example, a court may take into account whether the finder could have been expected to know that his find was treasure. I would have liked to spell out what is meant by reasonable excuse but was not allowed to do so by the lawyers, but obviously if someone fails to report a find because he made it the day before he went on holiday that would count. It is of course the case that this provision is not intended to be used to penalise innocent parties, but only those who wilfully fail to report their finds.

The Code of Practice continues that if finders are in any doubt as to whether any of the objects they have found are treasure they are advised to report them. The duty to report finds of treasure lies with the individual who made the find and this duty applies to everyone, including archaeologists. The Code contains suggestions about how this might be handled in the case of finds made during archaeological excavations (see below) and metal detecting rallies.

It is important to make it as easy as possible for finders to report their finds. The Code of Practice says that finders can report their finds in person, by letter, by fax or by telephone. The coroner will give or send the finder an acknowledgement that he has reported the find and will give instructions as to where the finder should deliver his find. This could be to the coroner himself or, in most instances, to a museum or to a local authority archaeological service. Before the Act comes into force the Department intends to have drawn up local agreements for each coroner's district in England and Wales between coroners, local government archaeological officers and museums as to how the arrangements for the delivery of finds of treasure will work and these will be publicised in leaflets. The Code of Practice recognises that the pilot schemes for the voluntary recording of finds will also have a valuable role to play here. In areas where such arrangements already exist, like Norfolk, archaeologists from the Museums Service attend all club meetings to identify and record finds. They also collect any finds that might be treasure trove. I hope that this is how the system will work across the country from 1999.

The Code notes that one aim of the agreements will be to ensure that appropriate archaeological advice is obtained as soon as possible and it stresses the importance of ensuring that the relevant SMR is informed about the find as soon as possible to see whether the find-spot should be investigated.

If the object is clearly not treasure in the opinion of the museum curator then they will be able to return it to the person that reported it. The museum curator will give his opinion to the coroner and it will not be necessary to take it any further. If it is necessary for the museum to take the find in the Code of Practice specifies what details should be included in the receipt given to the finder. A model receipt form will be circulated to all relevant museums and archaeological services who agree to provide advice on finds of treasure. The Code stresses the importance of keeping find-spots confidential, although of course finders should report them. We may expect that quite a lot of finds will be reported that will not be treasure - certainly at first - and it will be important to deal with these as quickly as possible.

If the curator believes that a find may be treasure they should inform the British Museum (or the National Museums & Galleries of Wales). Finds that no museum wishes to acquire can be disclaimed without an inquest. The local museum and national museum should agree whether to advise that the object should be disclaimed, after having consulted any other registered museums that they believe may have a potential interest in acquiring the find. If no museum wishes to acquire the find, then the national museum will advise that it be disclaimed, and will inform the coroner. Only a complete find (for example, a complete coin hoard) may be disclaimed in this way; if a museum wishes to acquire any objects from a find, then the whole find will need to be considered at a treasure inquest.

If a find is disclaimed, the coroner will then return it. He will notify the occupier and the landowner (if different) that he intends to return the object to the finder not less than twenty-eight days after the date of his notification unless he receives an objection. If he does receive an objection, the find will be retained by the coroner, or by the museum to whom he has entrusted it, pending the resolution of the dispute. The coroner does not have the power to decide whether the occupier, landowner or finder has the best claim to it, and this question will, if necessary, need to be resolved in the courts.

If any museum does wish to acquire the whole find or an object from the find, then the coroner will need to

hold an inquest and the national and local museums will prepare a report for the coroner. The British Museum (or the National Museums & Galleries of Wales) will also be able to provide specialist conservation and analytical facilities. It is the coroner's responsibility to make arrangements for the object to be delivered to the national museum. The report will give brief details of the objects together with an assessment as to whether they fall within the definition of treasure and, if so, on what grounds; it will not contain a valuation of the objects. In the case of objects other than coins, it may be necessary to obtain a scientific analysis, wherever possible without sampling, of one or more objects from the find in order to determine whether they fall within the definition of treasure under the Act. It will not normally be necessary to obtain an analysis of the metal content of coins. In some cases it may also be necessary to clean the objects so that they can be identified.

The coroner will have the duty of notifying the finder, the occupier and the owner of the land where the find was made of the inquest and they will be given an opportunity to examine witnesses and may be represented at it. The inquest will be held without a jury unless the coroner decides otherwise. The find-spot should be kept confidential.

If an object is found not to be treasure as a result of an inquest, then it will be returned by the coroner according to the principles set out on the return of objects that have been disclaimed.

If a find is declared treasure and if the coroner is advised that a museum may wish to acquire either the whole find or an object from it, the coroner shall arrange for the find to be delivered to the national museum so that it can be valued.

Finds of treasure made during the course of archaeological excavations
As noted above, the duty to report finds applies to objects found during archaeological excavations - obviously it is important that the new law should apply equally to all. However, in order to minimise any additional burden on archaeologists there is a special procedure for such finds. The Code of Practice states that one member of the excavation team may take the responsibility for informing the coroner and it also states that, according to the local arrangements that have been agreed in each coroner's district, it should normally be possible for the coroner to direct that the find should remain with the archaeological organisation concerned. That organisation will then need to inform the British

Museum or the National Museums & Galleries of Wales of any finds of treasure so that they will be able to recommend that they should be disclaimed without the need to hold an inquest. Lastly, the Code states that there is a presumption that objects of treasure found during the course of archaeological excavations will be kept with the rest of the archaeological archive.

Liability

The coroner or the body into whose care a find has been entrusted will take reasonable steps to ensure its safe custody and, in the event of an object being lost or damaged, except by the negligence of the party concerned, the Secretary of State may make an *ex gratia* payment to the person who would have been entitled to the reward, subject to a lower limit of £100.

Best practice for metal detectorists

The Code also contains a section on best practice for detectorists and, of course, these are recommendations only. Detectorists are urged to join a recognised metal detecting club or organisation but the Code recognises that special steps may have to be taken to draw the provisions of the Act to the attention of independent detectorists. Detectorists are also urged to abide by the National Council for Metal Detecting's Code of Conduct. The Code stresses that all those intending to search for objects or to undertake archaeological excavations must obtain the necessary permissions. It also recommends that anyone who intends to search for artefacts should make an agreement with the occupier and the landowner (if different) as to how any reward should be divided between them.

The Code states that if searching on cultivated land, metal detectorists should take care to recover items only from the plough-soil. If finders discover something large or unusual they are strongly recommended to obtain appropriate archaeological help (the Code contains a list of all SMRs). If, while removing it from the ground, a finder deliberately or recklessly causes significant damage to an object or to a surrounding monument, then this may result in a reduced reward. On the other hand, if a finder does not remove the whole of a find from the ground but reports it, thus affording the opportunity for the archaeological excavation of the remainder of the find, the original finder will normally be eligible for a reward for the whole find and not just that part which he himself had removed from the ground. This should serve as a strong incentive for detectorists to behave responsibly if they do make a major find. Archaeologists will not normally be eligible for rewards.

Finders are recommended, where possible, to note information such as where the find was made, how deep the find was, whether the find-spot is on cultivated land or under grass and anything else they have found or noticed in the ground (such as metal objects, pottery fragments or building rubble) in the surrounding area at the time of the discovery or previously.

Many detectorists complain that the reporting of finds can lead to the sites being given protection as scheduled ancient monuments and that the possibility of this would deter landowners from giving permission to search in the first place. The Code of Practice confirms that there is no known example where new detector finds on their own have led to a site being scheduled. Scheduling is carried out systematically under the Monuments Protection Programme, by which English Heritage is reviewing archaeological sites as potential candidates for scheduling. To qualify, a site must meet very stringent criteria in order to satisfy the Secretary of State, that in accordance with the legislation, it is of national importance, and that its management is best achieved by the controls of the scheduled monument consent system. Isolated detector finds on their own do not provide sufficient justification for scheduling, although such sites may be scheduled if other, more detailed, archaeological information about them exists. In any event, only a small proportion of the total number of known archaeological sites will be scheduled. At present there are about 17,000 scheduled monuments. This will increase to about 32,000 monuments when the Monuments Protection Programme is completed, but this will still represent less than 10% of the currently known monuments and find-spots.

The Code of Practice goes on to note that the great majority of known archaeological sites are not scheduled. Although there are no legal restrictions on metal detecting on such sites, the Government strongly recommends to all metal detectorists that, if they do find significant archaeological objects that are not treasure on a particular site, they should consult the local authority archaeologist or the local museum to ensure that they will not be causing damage or loss of archaeological evidence on a known archaeological site. It is recognised that there will be occasions where the reporting of finds by detectorists from unscheduled sites will lead to an archaeological investigation of the site and that such investigations may lead to the discovery of significant archaeological remains, so that it may be desirable to suspend further detecting on that site for a fixed period of time. Where this happens, archaeologists should ensure that the detectorist who originally reported the find is kept fully informed, by explaining to the finder what subsequent archaeological action will be taken, by sharing with them the new understanding that results from the find and by giving the original finder due acknowledgement for his discovery in any subsequent publication of the find. Archaeologists should give the finder the opportunity to be actively involved in any future archaeological investigation of the site where the find was made, wherever practicable. Archaeological bodies are urged to co-operate in this way because the logic of the pilot schemes for the voluntary recording of all archaeological finds is that they should be based on co-operation between archaeologists and metal detectorists.

On the question of the cleaning of objects, finders are recommended only to undertake the minimum amount of cleaning necessary to establish whether their find might be treasure and finds should not be cleaned further without the professional advice of an experienced archaeological conservator. The Code contains an Appendix which gives detailed guidance on the care of finds.

Valuations

The Code of Practice sets out revised guidelines for the valuation of finds of treasure which museums wish to acquire. At present the independent Treasure Trove Reviewing Committee advises the Secretary of State on these valuations and their role is to determine the full market value of the objects. We believe that one of the great strengths of the British system of treasure trove is that finders who behave properly can expect to receive the full market value of their finds if a museum acquires them and the Code of Practice proposes that the Committee is to be retained, but renamed the Treasure Valuation Committee.

Under the old system, the British Museum or the National Museums & Galleries of Wales used to submit valuation reports to the Committee and the Committee could then take further advice if it thought it necessary. The Code of Practice proposes that the national museums will no longer submit valuation reports and instead the Committee will commission reports in all cases from independent experts drawn from the trade. Finders and museums will be able to comment on these valuations before the Committee makes its recommendation and finders will continue to be able to commission their own reports, as they can at present. The whole logic of

these reforms is to provide the greatest possible transparency in the decision making process.

Acquisition of finds

Once a find has been declared treasure there then arises the question of which museum should acquire it. At present the practice is that the British Museum (or the National Museums & Galleries of Wales) have the right to acquire treasure troves and if they do not wish to acquire the find they then offer it to local museums. This does not mean that all finds go to the national museum: over the last three years there were seventy-eight treasure troves: the British Museum acquired sixteen finds intact and selected coins from a further nine hoards. Other museums acquired objects from a total of thirty-five treasure troves. The Code of Practice states that this system should continue but sets out for the first time the criteria to be followed by the British Museum or the National Museums & Galleries of Wales in deciding whether to acquire a find of treasure and states that the national museum should consult the local museum before making its decision. It also says that there is a presumption in favour of acquiring finds intact. There was some criticism of this part of the Code of Practice and some local museums suggested that the job of allocating finds be given to a committee. The problem with this is that the Treasure Trove Reviewing Committee would not be suitable since anyone with a museum connection is specifically excluded from that Committee, so it would have meant setting up a second committee which would have been excessively bureaucratic. This issue will be looked at again in the review that will take place after three years.

Rewards

On the payment of rewards, the Code of Practice aims to strike a balance between interests of finder, occupier and landowner. The responses that received from the consultation exercise suggest that we have achieved this. To summarise, the Code of Practice states that:

- where the finder has permission to be on the land, rewards should continue to be paid in full to him; the burden of proof as to whether he has permission will rest with the finder

- if the finder makes an agreement with the occupier or landowner to share a reward, the Secretary of State will be prepared to follow the terms of the agreement

- where the finder has committed an offence in relation to a find, or has trespassed, or has not followed best practice as set out in the Code of Practice, he or she may expect no reward at all or a reduced reward

- landowners and occupiers will for the first time be eligible for rewards in such cases

- archaeologists will not normally be eligible for rewards

- and lastly the Code of Practice defines the respective interests of landowner and occupier in cases where they are eligible for rewards

Initiative for the voluntary recording of all archaeological finds

Personally I think that this initiative is potentially considerably more important than the Act, and yet I am also sure that it could never have happened without it. As members of the SMA will know all too well, there is a long history to this issue, as archaeologists have been pressing the Government to take action for many years. In March 1996 the Department of National Heritage published a discussion document on Portable Antiquities. This paper made a distinction between two aspects of the problem: the public acquisition of finds, which the Treasure Act addresses, and the recording of finds, which is what the proposals on portable antiquities are intended to tackle. The discussion paper quoted a survey by the Council for British Archaeology which attempted to quantify the precise number of objects being found (Dobinson and Denison 1995). It is very difficult to be precise, and only a few metal detectorists co-operated, but it is estimated that several hundred thousand archaeological objects are being found each year, maybe around 400,000. Of these, only a very small percentage, no more than about 5-10%, are seen by museums. To give an example of the scale of the problem: in Norfolk a voluntary agreement between metal detectorists and Norwich Museum has been running for several years. Around 20,000 objects a year are recorded and the equivalent of three members of staff are employed on this. The document confirmed that the Government accepts that there is an urgent need for action.

The discussion document then discussed the relative merits of voluntary and compulsory schemes. Under a voluntary system, the Government would draw up, in consultation with representatives of museums and archaeological organisations and also of metal detectorists, a voluntary scheme for the recording of archaeological objects found in England and Wales. One of the advantages of such an approach is that it would not require legislation and thus it could be introduced with the minimum of delay and the document states that the Government's provisional view is that a voluntary scheme offers the best solution and it invited comments from interested parties.

A compulsory duty to report all archaeological objects would in any case have required fresh legislation, which would have cut across the logic of the Treasure Act, and it would have required very substantial additional resources in order to operate such a system.

A total of 174 responses were received, roughly equally divided between archaeological and metal detecting interests. Everyone who responded agreed on the importance of recording archaeological finds and on the need to improve the current arrangements, while the balance of opinion was strongly in favour of a voluntary rather than a compulsory system. This means that for the first time there was a broad consensus for the way in which this should be taken forward.

In December 1996, the Department announced that it would establish a two year programme of pilot schemes to commence on 1 September 1997 and it will make £50,000 available for the seven-month period that falls within the year 1997-98 (see Appendix 2 of the Code of Practice). The scheme will be co-ordinated directly by this Department and the funding will be channelled through the Museums and Galleries Commission. The aim of the pilot schemes will be to enable an accurate estimate to be made of the resources that would be needed to extend the scheme across the whole of England. The funding will be directed towards employing additional staff in up to five areas to record finds. The first step was to invite any suitable body to express an interest in bidding for funding. In fact we received a very strong response with over fifty bids from organisations covering virtually the entire country. This clearly indicates the support in the museums and archaeological world for such a scheme. The grants were announced on 1 June 1997: full-time posts will be established at Kent County Council (for a scheme to cover the whole county, in co-operation with the relevant museums and detecting clubs); Norfolk Museums Service (one of the responsibilities of this post will be to carry out a study of how the system for recording finds in Norfolk has worked over the last twenty years); Liverpool Museum (for a post to cover a large area of the north-west); a post shared between the Yorkshire Museum and the York Archaeological Trust and lastly a part-time post at North Lincolnshire District Museum. In addition, the British Museum subsequently agreed to provide funding for an additional full-time post and, following further consultation, it was announced in July that this money would go to a bid submitted by the West Midlands Archaeological Collections Research Unit for a post based at the West Midlands Regional Museums Council.

The pilot schemes only represent the first stage of the project. Providing that they can be seen to produce worthwhile results - and I have every expectation that they will, as the example of Norfolk shows what can be done - I hope it will be possible to move to a national scheme when the pilots come to an end in 1999. One of the main aims of the pilots will be to enable one to make an accurate estimate of the level of resources needed for a national scheme. However, we can already begin to make some tentative estimates and it is likely that around forty additional posts might be needed in all. At present I do not know where the funding for this is going to come from: I am approaching this exercise one step at a time. But I feel that it is an obvious candidate for lottery funding and I think that the prospects are quite encouraging.

This project has enormous potential and the Department has said that it sees these proposals as important in their way as the Treasure Act. If 400,000 new finds a year can be recorded this will soon develop into a most important new resource for the understanding of this country's past. The archaeological and academic potential is enormous, but that is just one part of it. It will also be essential to demonstrate public support for the scheme and it will be vital to show that this information is not being gathered just for the benefit of archaeologists and academic researchers but that it will be a highly important new source for the history of this country. I think that this will be possible both through the imaginative use of computer technology to make the information publicly accessible and also perhaps through a programme of publications making use of the information. I am certain that this co-operation between archaeologists and detectorists must be the way forward and I believe that together this Act and the voluntary scheme offer a golden opportunity for detectorists and archaeologists to make a fresh start to everyone's benefit.

APPENDIX 1

Portable antiquities legislation in European countries

Summary
This comparative survey shows very clearly that the legal protection afforded portable antiquities in England and Wales is at the same time more limited in scope and more permissive and also more liberal in its treatment of finders than in virtually any other country in Europe.

To take the four categories separately, as regards the duty to report finds, only Belgium has a weaker requirement than England and Wales, where in practice only finds likely to qualify as Treasure Trove have to be reported (ie, essentially hoards of precious metal coins and other objects), although legally all gold and silver objects should be reported. The great majority of other countries, including other parts of the United Kingdom (Scotland and Northern Ireland), have legislation requiring the reporting of all archaeological finds. The Treasure Act will only make a very minor adjustment to the current reporting requirement in England and Wales.

Similarly, all countries except Belgium provide legal protection to a much wider range of objects than England. In most countries the State can either claim ownership of or have the right to pre-empt all significant archaeological finds. When viewed against this background, the Treasure Act will only widen the Crown's rights in a very modest way.

England's practice of paying the finder the full market value as assessed by an independent committee is more liberal than most countries, in many of which the reward bears little relation to the market value, while in some only the landowner is eligible for a reward.

Lastly, in most countries all archaeological excavation is controlled and metal detectors can only be used under licence and these are not normally given to treasure hunters. The only exceptions are some of the Scandinavian countries (Denmark, Norway and Finland). In England, Wales and Scotland, metal detecting is only controlled on scheduled ancient monuments.

Sources
Hill 1936 (England, Wales and all other countries before 1936); Sheridan 1995 (Scotland); Kelly 1995 (Ireland); Burnham 1974; Prott and O'Keefe 1984; Prott and O'Keefe 1988; Council of Europe 1981; UNESCO, n.d.; UNESCO 1987a, 1987b and 1988

Country	Reporting Requirements	Ownership	Rewards	Metal Detectors	Date of Legislation
England & Wales	Legal requirement to report only those finds defined as Treasure (see next panel). Reporting of other finds to be dealt with through a voluntary scheme.	The following categories are treasure and belong to Crown:(a) all hoards of coins at least 300 years old (except for hoards of fewer than 10 base metal coins); (b) all objects other than coins at least 300 years old which have a precious-metal content of at least 5%; (c) associated objects are treasure.	If Treasure, finder to receive reward equivalent to market value as assessed by independent committee. Landowner will be eligible if finder is trespassing.	No licenses required. No restrictions except on scheduled ancient Monuments (some 25,000 in England and Wales).	1979; 1996
Scotland	All ownerless objects to be reported.	All ownerless objects belong to Crown under *bona vacantia*. (This subsumes the law of Treasure Trove which also exists and is wider in scope than in England and Wales.) All finds legally required to be reported. In practice Crown only claims those objects that it decides are important.	If claimed by Crown, finder receives reward equivalent to market value as assessed by independent committee. Landowner not eligible.	As in England and Wales. (Scotland has some 6,200 scheduled monuments)	
Northern Ireland	All archaeological objects to be reported; Crown can retain them for up to 3 months.	Treasure Act applies.	If TT, finder receives reward equivalent to market value as assessed by independent committee.	Licence required to search for archaeological objects (1937 legislation, renewed in 1995): not normally given to treasure hunters. Use or possession of metal detectors on scheduled monuments an offence (1995 legislation).	1995
Republic of Ireland	All archaeological objects.	All archaeological objects are the property of the state. It is an offence to own or trade archaeological objects from the soil of the Republic. The law contained retrospective provisions requiring all privately owned antiquities with Irish provenances to be reported within 3 months of enactment.	Finder receives reward (normally less than market value). Treasure hunters not rewarded.	Licence required to search for archaeological objects: never given to treasure hunters. Metal detecting magazines banned.	1987 & 1994
France	All archaeological finds to be reported.	State has right of pre-emption of all such finds.	Compensation to be agreed between parties concerned (expert opinion may be sought); reward split equally between landowner and finder.	Licence required to search for archaeological objects; not normally given to treasure hunters.	1941
Belgium (Wallonia)	All archaeological finds to be reported within 8 days.	State has no right to acquire objects.	Title belongs equally to landowner and finder.	An offence to use a metal detector for archaeological purposes except for officially authorised excavations.	1991

Belgium (Flemish region)	All archaeological finds to be reported within 3 days.	State has no right to acquire objects.	Title belongs equally to landowner and finder.	An offence to use a metal detector to search for archaeological objects except for officially authorised excavations. Anyone with archaeological qualifications may obtain a licence.	1993 - 5
Luxembourg	All archaeological objects whether found during excavation or as chance finds to be reported.	(to be confirmed)	(to be confirmed)	Licence required to search for archaeological objects, including metal detecting; sometimes given to treasure hunters.	1991
Netherlands	All finds to be reported.	If object is more than 50 years old and of artistic, research or historical interest it is classed as a monument and State has right of pre-emption.	Finder and landowner to share full market value equally (finder is not rewarded if an archaeologist).	(to be confirmed)	1988 & 1992
Germany (each Land has its own legislation; in general these follow the following pattern)	All archaeological finds to be reported.	State generally has right to acquire all finds of historic value.	Finder and landowner to share reward.	Licence required to search for archaeological objects; not normally given to treasure hunters.	Various
Austria	All chance finds to be reported.	Legal protection afforded "monuments": that is movable and immovable property of historical, artistic or cultural importance whose preservation is a matter of public interest.	(to be confirmed)	Licence required to search for archaeological objects; not normally given to treasure hunters.	1923
Italy	All chance finds or finds from excavations to be reported.	All objects of historical or archaeological interest found by chance or during excavation belong to State.	Finder and landowner each entitled to a quarter of the value of the find, or else to part of the find if the State so decides.	Licence required to search for archaeological objects; not given to treasure hunters.	1939
Malta	All finds to be reported.	Legal protection afforded to all objects of archaeological or antiquarian importance.	(to be confirmed)	Licence required to search for archaeological objects; not given to treasure hunters. Import of metal detectors banned since 1979.	1925 & 1974
Spain	All finds to be reported.	All finds of the Spanish Historical Heritage (i.e., all archaeological objects) are the property of the State.	Finder and landowner each entitled to one quarter of the value.	Licence required to search for archaeological objects; not given to treasure hunters.	1985
Portugal	(to be confirmed)	State has right of pre-emption over all cultural objects.	(to be confirmed)	(to be confirmed)	1985

Greece	All finds to be reported.	All finds the property of the State. They may be left in the possession of the holder if they are of little scientific significance, but their transfer must be reported. State has right of pre-emption from dealers.	If found on private land, landowner receives one half of the value. If found on State or Church land by an employee, finder finder receives half its value.	Licence required to search for archaeological objects; not given to treasure hunters.	1932
Cyprus	All objects made before 1700 to be reported.	State has right of pre-emption to all objects made before 1700; their transfer has to be reported to the State.	(to be confirmed)	Licence required to search for archaeological objects; not given to treasure hunters.	1935 & 1959
Denmark	All "objects o f the past including coins" to be reported.	All such objects shall be treasure trove and belong to the State.	Finder to receive reward based on value of the material, rarity of find and care with which finder has safeguarded find.	Licence required for use of metal detectors; all finds to be reported to landowner and museum.	1984-9
Sweden	All finds over 100 years old to be reported.	All objects found on an ancient monument State property. If found elsewhere and at least 100 years old, objects the property of the finder. If the finds contain metal objects or two or more objects deposited together then the State has the right of pre-emption.	Finder is rewarded. For finds of gold and silver he receives the value of the metal plus one-eighth; for finds of copper, the scientific value of the object.	Licence required: not given to treasure hunters.	1988
Norway	All antiquities (as defined opposite) to be reported.	Wide range of specified categories of movable objects made before 1537 (for coins, before 1650) belong to State.	Reward to be divided equally between finder and landowner. If made of gold or silver reward equivalent to value of metal plus 10%.	No specific restrictions but certain scheduled sites are protected	1978
Finland	Archaeological objects more than 100 years old to be reported.	State has right of pre-emption of such objects.	Finders rewarded at discretion of Archaeological Commission. Reward is fixed as the metal value plus 25% .	No restrictions	1963
Israel	All objects made before 1700 to be reported	All objects made before 1700 the property of the State (though the State may choose to disclaim objects).	If it keeps the object, the State may reward the finder at its discretion.	Licence is required: not given to treasure hunters.	1978

17

References

Anon 1994 The Good, the Bad and the Understaffed. The National Monuments Amendment Bill 1993 *Archaeology Ireland News* 8, 1 (Spring, 1994), 5

Bland, R 1996 Treasure trove and the case for reform *Art, Antiquity and Law* I 1 (February 1996) 11-26

Bland, R 1997 Amersham, Buckinghamshire: 7 nummi to AD 378 in R Bland and J Orna-Ornstein (eds) *Coin Hoards from Roman Britain* X British Museum Press, 410

Bland, R and Burnett, A M 1988 Normanby, Lincolnshire: 47909 radiates to 289 in *Coin Hoards from Roman Britain* 8, British Museum Press, 114-215

Burnham, B 1974 *The Protection of Cultural Property. A Handbook of National Legislations* ICOM

Carey Miller, D L and Sheridan, A 1997, Treasure trove in Scots law *Art, Antiquity and Law* forthcoming

Carman, J 1996 *Valuing Ancient Things* Leicester University Press

Cherry, J 1994 *The Middleham Jewel and Ring* The Yorkshire Museum

Cleere, H 1991 The law relating to ownership and archaeological collecting in England and Wales *The Museum Archaeologist* 16, 30-34

Cleere, H 1994 The CBA: the first fifty years in *Council for British Archaeology Report No. 44*, 108-9

Council of Europe 1981 *Metal Detectors and Archaeology. Report of the Committee on Culture and Education* Council of Europe, Parliamentary Assembly, Doc. 4741, Strasbourg

Dobinson, C and Denison, S 1995 *Metal Detecting and Archaeology in England* English Heritage/Council for British Archaeology

Hill, G F 1936 *Treasure Trove in Law and Practice* Oxford

Hill, P V 1975 The Treasure Trove inquest in R L S Bruce-Mitford *The Sutton Hoo Ship-Burial* I, British Museum Publications, 718-31

Johns, C M 1997 *The Snettisham Roman Jeweller's Hoard* British Museum Press

Johns, C M and Potter, T W 1983 *The Thetford Treasure* British Museum Press

Kelly, E A 1995 Protecting Ireland's archaeological heritage, in Tubb 1995, 235-43

Longworth, I H 1992 Snettisham Revisited *International Journal of Cultural Property* 2, 1, 333-41

O'Connell, M G and Bird, J 1994 The Roman temple at Wanborough, excavation 1985-1986 *Surrey Archaeological Collections* 82, 1-168

Palmer, N 1993 Treasure Trove and Title to Discovered Antiquities *International Journal of Cultural Property* 2, 2, 275-318

Prott, L V and O'Keefe, P J 1984 *Law and the Cultural Heritage, Volume 1. Discovery and Excavation* Abingdon

Prott, L V and O'Keefe, P J 1988 *Handbook of National Regulations concerning the Export of Cultural Property* UNESCO, Paris

Renfrew 1995 Letter in *Museums Journal* October 1995, 18

Schadla-Hall, T 1994 Antiquities legislation: A proper basis? in *The Museum Archaeologist* 21, 12-16

Schadla-Hall, T 1995a Letter in *Museums Journal* September 1995, 18

Schadla-Hall, T 1995b Letter in *Museums Journal* December 1995, 16

Selkirk, A 1994a Treasure Bill *Current Archaeology* 137 (February/March 1994), 177

Selkirk, A 1994b Nationalising our past *Current Archaeology* 138 (April/May 1994), 214

Sheridan, A 1991 What's mine is Her Majesty's - The law in Scotland *The Museum Archaeologist* 16, 35-40

Sheridan, A 1994 The Scottish "Treasure Trove" system: A suitable case for emulation? *The Museum Archaeologist* 21, 4-11

Sheridan, A 1995 Portable antiquities legislation in Scotland: what is it, and how well does it work? in Tubb 1995, 193-204

Stead, I M 1991 The Snettisham excavations in 1990 *Antiquity* 65, 447-64

Tubb, K 1995 (ed.) *Antiquities, Trade or Betrayed* Archetype

UNESCO, n. d. *The Protection of Movable Cutural Property, I. Compendium of Legislative Texts* (Austria, Belgium, France, Poland)

UNESCO 1987a *The Protection of Movable Cutural Property. Collection of Legislative Texts: Norway*

UNESCO 1987b *The Protection of Movable Cutural Property. Collection of Legislative Texts: Greece*

UNESCO 1988 *The Protection of Movable Cutural Property. Collection of Legislative Texts: Spain*

Ward, A 1994 Treasure Trove: challenging the decisions of coroner's courts *International Journal of Cultural Property* 1, 3, 121-4

THE ST ALBANS URBAN ARCHAEOLOGICAL STRATEGY PROJECT

Isobel Thompson, St Albans District Council

This is one of a series of projects currently being funded by English Heritage in thirty-two historic towns and cities in England, and is being carried out for the Planning Department of St Albans District Council. These projects are intended to enable PPG 16 to be implemented efficiently in major historic urban centres, where there are both rich archaeological remains and continuing development pressure. Each project involves three phases: database, assessment and strategy.

The detailed proposal for St Albans was drawn up by the District Archaeologist, Rosalind Niblett. The aim is to provide an accurate assessment of the archaeological resource in St Albans, in an easily accessible form, which is capable of being sorted, cross-referenced and compared. The main day to day use of the database is as a planning aid, to provide background information for committee reports, and for use in preparing recommendations to the relevant committee concerning the determination of planning applications. The database is also a valuable research tool.

English Heritage and RCHME have drawn up a data standard manual for these databases (RCHME/EH Urban Databases Data Standards and Compilers Manual), but it is intended to be adapted to suit local requirements; only some of the fields are mandatory, some are recommended and some are optional. The key feature of these databases is that separate records are made for archaeological 'events' (excavations and other observations) and for 'monuments', with cross-referencing between the two. This has proved a good way to cope with the complexity of archaeological information in towns.

The database phase ran from April 1995 to July 1996. One person (myself) was employed full-time for this period to gather and input the data, and one half-time illustrator was employed, also on a contract, to map each event and monument on the District Council GIS. She was a geologist, with an archaeology O-level and local knowledge, and was admirably suited to the job as she understood what we were doing and could cope with the vagaries of the GIS. The District Council system is not a very up-to-date package and neither it nor the

computer system is Windows-based. The IT section drew up in-house software for the database itself. From the beginning it was the intention to map each archaeological event (outlining each excavation trench where possible) and each monument, but not to extend the mapping to anything else at this stage.

The compilation took a defined route. First came the listing of sources, everything that could be located: published, archive, personal reminiscences, drawings, letters, manuscripts. From examination of these sources all events were recorded. Their definition is given in the manual as 'any event, observation or activity which has enabled information to be gathered or a judgement to be made about the archaeological resource in a particular locality, whether surviving or destroyed.' In effect this is any circumstance (from verbal memory of an observation to full excavation) which can be dated and mapped, at least approximately, and which provided archaeological information. Each event record includes details of who did the work and when; where the finds and records are kept; the sources of information; and a list of the elements using the county SMR generic terms: the presence of pits, wells, ovens, tessellated pavements, cremations, or whatever, and how many of them. It will be possible to pull up, say, all the tessellated pavements within the database area, or excavated organic materials, or Roman inhumations, and this facility should be of particular use to researchers and museum staff.

The next stage was to compile a record of all monuments discernible from these events. A monument is any 'single period structure or complex having a specific function, purpose or symbolic meaning'. This is easier to define in practice than it sounds and presented no particular problems. Each event and each monument was given a unique number and mapped on the GIS. This mapping is the end result of the compilation and the starting point for enquiries. Given the available resources, we are happy with the result.

The project covers twelve one-kilometre squares of the National Grid: TL 120 to 160 Easting, and TL 060 to 090 Northing. An arbitrary boundary (rather than an historical one) means that it is easy to establish what is covered by the database: nothing outside these grid squares is included. They cover rather more than the urban area (which includes urban Verulamium, half of which is a municipal park). As a result they include the prehistoric settlement areas of Prae Wood; the whole of Verulamium including the Fosse; the abbey precinct; the medieval town and parts of the Gorhambury estate. The dateline was fixed at AD 1600, which kept the project manageable but included the post-Dissolution upheaval. The procedure was to take advantage of what was thought to be the unique nature of settlement in St Albans, an apparent succession of new sites, and to divide the area into sections. We began with the small area of Kingsbury, known as the site of the Saxon burh, to use it to test the software and make any necessary changes; prehistoric Prae Wood followed, then the abbey precinct (a larger area), the Roman town (by far the largest area), and finally the medieval town.

This proved a practical approach, which was just as well, as there turned out to be a far larger number of events and monuments than was estimated for the project proposal. We were surprised at the sheer quantity dredged up by examining everything we could find and also at the amount which could be mapped (a basic requirement). This itself shows how the archaeological resource in the city may be underestimated. The compilation of all discoverable data was one of the prime aims of the whole project, so that the best advice can be given on the archaeological resource, whether to planners, archaeologists, or museum staff. The subject of any serious enquiry can be traced from the GIS plan, via the database itself, to the paper files for each event and monument and ultimately back to the original sources. By this route the quality of the database record, and any value judgements made in the process by the compiler, can be assessed. It seems vital that this should be possible.

The bringing together of a vast and disparate body of data has meant that advice could be given on planning applications in each area as soon as it was completed. The mapping kept pace with the data compilation and detailed advice on the location of the archaeological resource could be given. But it is also intended that the database should be available to aid research. The District Archaeologist drew up a list of research objectives as part of the database proposal. Further research and publication projects have suggested themselves during the gathering of the data and certainly more could be identified. The information contained in the database is available to all genuine researchers, while the need to safeguard the heritage will be protected by the adoption of the guidelines currently used by Hertfordshire County Council in connection with the county SMR.

The next phase in the project is to use the database to produce an academic assessment, synthesising and summarising the data gathered and setting out the current knowledge of the town. This phase began in September 1996 and will take eleven months with publication in view. By this means the detailed statement of our current knowledge should reach as many people as possible, and will be readily available.

The Assessment will in turn be used as the basis for an Urban Strategy Document, setting out the strategy, policies and planning proposals that will be adopted in St Albans in order to manage the archaeological resources in its urban core.

The close examination of original sources for the archaeological events, particularly early ones, and the mapping requirement, meant that a certain amount of re-assessment was inevitable even in the first phase. The academic assessment will deal with each period in turn, with a separate section for the abbey precinct, which has not been studied as an entity since 1876. I am writing most of these chapters; Rosalind Niblett will write the section on Roman Verulamium, a huge task in itself, and sections on deposit analysis and a general evaluation for each period using her own long experience.

Some very interesting results have already emerged, perhaps most notably the demonstration that the Saxon burh was very probably not where it has been assumed to lie since 1905. The mapping of all presently available information on 5th to 11th century St Albans, together with a close look at the Victorian ideas behind the 1905 paper that fixed the Saxon burh in present-day Kingsbury, has instead indicated a battle for jurisdiction between the abbey on the hill top and the old settlement in a decayed Verulamium in the valley bottom. Since the late Iron Age settlement pattern now appears to be that of a circle of enclosures on the higher ground around a focal point in the valley bottom, where the Roman forum was to be built, the history of settlement in St Albans is clearly no longer to be considered unique. It is not the story of a succession of new sites after all, but the movement from one early focus in the valley, to another founded by the abbey on the hilltop and promoted with some ruthlessness at the beginning of the eleventh century.

MANAGING WINCHESTER'S ARCHAEOLOGICAL RESOURCE

Richard Whinney, Winchester Museums Service

In 1992, English Heritage launched a major initiative whose avowed purpose was to propose a framework for the future management of the archaeological heritage of thirty or so historic towns in England (English Heritage 1992). For each town or city, a three stage approach to the comprehensive management of the urban archaeological resource is suggested. The three stages are:

Urban Archaeological Database (UAD): the compilation of an up-to-date and comprehensive computerised database of information about the urban archaeological resource.

Urban Archaeological Assessment (UAA): compilation of a document which synthesises and summarises our current knowledge and understanding of the archaeological resource, drawing heavily on the UAD. These assessments are seen as providing the basis for the Urban Archaeology Strategy document.

Urban Archaeology Strategy (UAS): compilation of a document which sets out strategies for managing the urban archaeological resource of particular historic towns or cities. The document is to be based on the UAA, but will also take into account such factors as local and national development policies, planning proposals and so forth. It is clear that the Urban Archaeology Strategy will require periodic updating, in the light of changing archaeological information, or in response to changes in planning policies and guidance.

Winchester is one of the thirty historic towns identified by English Heritage. This paper describes the progress so far made towards the development and implementation of Winchester's Urban Archaeological Strategy.

The Urban Archaeology Database
Initial discussions began with English Heritage in April 1993, which resulted in several project designs being presented, modified and finally agreed in December 1993. Work on the UAD began in earnest in the summer of 1994 and was substantially completed by December 1995, with one person working full time on data gathering and verification, sites and monuments definitions, etc - a total of about eighteen months work.

Unlike some of the other historic towns, Winchester began the compilation of the UAD with the advantage of already having in place a substantially complete, although rather out of date, computerised sites and monuments record. This SMR had last been formally updated in the mid 1980s under the auspices of a Manpower Services Commission scheme. Although requiring substantial modification and up-dating, it provided the essential basis for the project.

The Study Area
The definition of the study area was the subject of some initial discussions but it was finally decided that the area to be covered would comprise the present Winchester City electoral wards. The area thereby defined (Fig 1), some 1545 hectares, includes not only the historic core and suburbs of the city, but also something of the surrounding chalk downlands, which are seen as important in providing a wider, more rural, background for the urban and suburban data.

Moreover, by using these local administrative boundaries to delimit the study area, straight forward correlation and co-operation with other local government departments, especially Planning, is greatly facilitated.

Methods and Standards
All the data was collected and verified using the recommended RCHME/EH data standards and structures(RCHME/English Heritage 1993)), with one or two extra fields added to make record completion more useful for Winchester.

There are two main linked or related databases:

The sites database, in which each recognition event ,or individual archaeological record, ranging from a large multi-period large scale excavation to a chance find of an artefact, is recorded.

The monuments database, in which either a single recognition event or a number of recognition events are interpreted as forming an entity defined as a monument.

Fig 1 The Winchester UAD study area (scale 1:30000).

The basic database structures for both recognition events and monuments, were constructed as suggested in the RCHME/EH standards, in order to facilitate eventual transfer of some data to the National Archaeological Record at Swindon

Sources of Evidence

A number of sources of evidence were investigated, and data from these sources is included in the Winchester UAD. In summary these sources are:

Sites and Monuments Records - Winchester SMR (see above), Hampshire County Council SMR

Post 1972 Excavation Archives - all types of archaeological intervention such as full excavations, salvage work, observations, evaluations, etc undertaken by the Archaeology Section of Winchester Museums Service since 1972. Because of the large quantities and complexity of the data, detailed archaeological information from each major intervention is held in a separate but linked Related Database

Boreholes and archaeological sections records - information on depth and nature of deposits from traditional engineering borehole logs and archaeological sections. This data is required as the basis for the deposit modelling elements of the UAA

Winchester Research Unit records - archaeological data from published sources and from archives relating to the series of major investigations carried out in Winchester between 1961 and 1971 by the Winchester Excavations Committee

Pictorial Sources - information, mainly about buildings, from early plans and other illustrations, and from photographs

Documentary sources - mainly summary information from Keene's tenement histories of Winchester from 1300 to 1550

Listed building information - data on buildings as available from the listed buildings registers for Winchester.

Summary

At the outset of the project it was estimated that the UAD would eventually contain about 3200 separate entries or recognition events (Fig 2), with about 330-350 monuments (Fig 3) being recognised. The actual number of recognition events is 4825 and 450 monuments have been defined. Clearly these figures are not final and are expected to increase gradually over time, as new recognition events are entered and new monuments defined.

Computerisation

Although not originally conceived of as such, the advantages of an integrated database and Geographical Information System (GIS) quickly became obvious, and the Winchester UAD is now a fully computerised system. The software in use for data storage and manipulation is *dBaseIV*, a commercially available relational database. Ordnance Survey digital data, which provides the modern topographical background to the UAD, is displayed and manipulated by a commercial package called *GGP Windows*. Although providing many of the facilities and functions of a full GIS, GGP Windows is not a fully fledged GIS package. However, for the limited area of the Winchester UAD, this is not a problem. The package was chosen because of its ease of use, and its cost, and for the company's commitment to regular upgrades and improvements. A further important factor in choosing GGP Windows is that the software is in use by the Local Planning Authority and exchange of data and information is therefore quite straightforward.

GGP Windows and dBaseIV together produce an almost seamless interface which allows considerable interaction and interchange of data, either on-screen or via printouts and other hard copy.

The UAD is easily stored and manipulated on a standard desktop Personal Computer, with a 17" graphics screen, linked to a colour printer and plotter. However, both GGP Windows and dBaseIV support networking functions, and so the information is potentially available to a large number of users at any time.

Data Exchange

One of the principles enshrined in the compilation of the UAD is the capacity for the exchange of data between Winchester and the National Monuments Record Centre in Swindon. Discussions are currently taking place about the format and content of the data to be exchanged (September 1997). Whilst it is envisaged that there will be no difficulty with the physical transfer, there is still some work to be done in order that copyright issues are resolved.

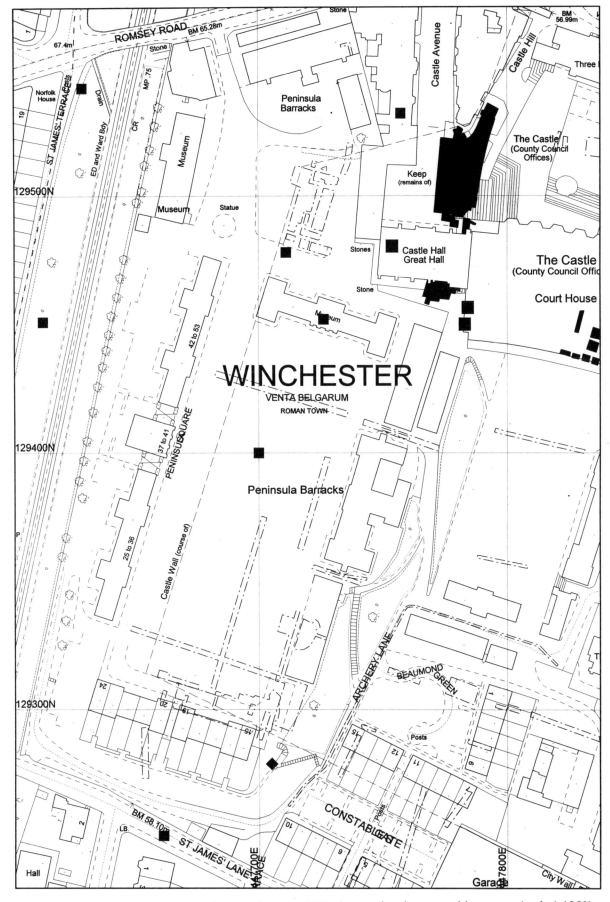

Fig 2 Printout of the Peninsula Barracks area of Winchester, showing recognition events (scale 1:1250)

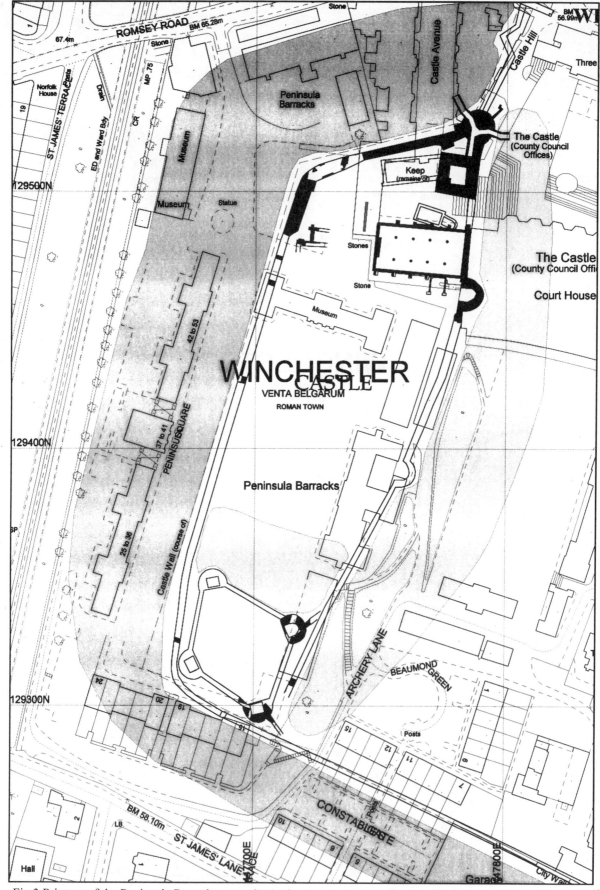

Fig 3 Printout of the Peninsula Barracks area of Winchester, showing medieval monuments (scale 1:1250)

The Urban Archaeology Assessment

Following the successful completion of the UAD, discussions and further consultations have taken place with English Heritage. These discussions have centred on how best to proceed from the UAD to the structure and compilation of the UAA, and on what the UAA should contain to be a useful document. The research design for the Assessment has just been agreed, and work has begun (September 1997).

Once completed, it is envisaged that the UAA for Winchester will be an up-to-date, point-in-time detailed assessment and consideration of present knowledge and understanding of Winchester's archaeology and history from earliest times to about AD1550. Although there will be some consideration of the periods after AD1550, these post-medieval and modern periods are the subject of a separate detailed study by the History Department of King Alfred's University College in Winchester, which is also developing its own database

The UAA will be a major document which sets out the known data for each of a series of broad chronological periods and which places each data set into a local, regional (and if appropriate national and international) archaeological and historical context.

The UAA will also include elements of deposit modelling, based upon both archaeological and engineering (borehole) data, to provide something of a three-dimensional picture of the location, extent and depth of surviving archaeological levels. Again this study will be broken into a number of broad chronological periods.

It is expected that in combination, the archaeological data and the deposit modelling data will produce for the first time, a period-by-period statement and synthesis of the current knowledge and understanding of Winchester's archaeological and historical resource.

Once completed, this synthesis will provide the basic information for a series of analyses and evaluations of the importance, potential and sensitivity of the archaeological and historical resource for each of the broad chronological periods.

The majority of the work required to produce the assessment will quite logically be undertaken by the staff of Winchester Museums Service who are the best placed to carry out such a task. However, it has been recognised from the outset that a wider viewpoint on some aspects of the UAA would be necessary. In particular, in the analyses and assessments of the importance, potential or sensitivity of the archaeological resource, a wider knowledge and understanding of data and information from regional, national and international contexts may be relevant. To this end, advice, comment, and input will be sought from outside academic sources at this stage of the project.

Assessment Outline

As currently conceived, the Urban Archaeological Assessment for Winchester will comprise the following four main sections (excluding Bibliography, Appendices and Gazetteers):

1. Introduction and Background: general introduction; past work and the nature of the evidence; geology, natural topography, soils and drainage; geomorphological change and environmental evidence.

2. Chronological and Deposit Models: the chronological model will explain and justify the periodisation adopted for the assessment; the deposit model will present information in a series of three-dimensional illustrations which will attempt to show the location, extent and depth of archaeological deposits for the Roman, Saxon and medieval periods.

3. Period Studies: the largest and most detailed section will include, for each chronological period, information on: historical framework, past work and nature of the evidence, description of the evidence, current state of knowledge and understanding; including lack of data/knowledge, and an assessment of importance and potential.

The chronological periods will be: prehistoric (palaeolithic to Bronze Age); Iron Age and early Roman; Venta Belgarum - the *civitas* capital; the "Dark Ages"; early medieval revival; medieval Winchester; the later medieval town (to 1550); the post-medieval and modern city (brief summary only).

Description and discussion of each of the periods will be accompanied by a series of plans depicting relevant information. All such plans will be generated directly from the UAD/GGP system. They will be presented at consistent scales throughout.

4. Syntheses and Assessment: current state of knowledge and understanding, being a summary and synthesis of the relevant parts of the Periods section, drawing out themes and ideas which may cut across the Period divisions; assessment of importance and potential, being a summary and synthesis of the relevant parts of the Periods sections.

The Future

It is projected that it will take about a year (from September 1997) to complete the assessment of Winchester's archaeological resource, based on the criteria outlined above. The final document will form the basis for the development of a comprehensive strategy for the management of the archaeological resource (UAS), principally through the planning process. The exact mechanisms for the structure and operation of the strategy have yet to be finalised, but it is envisaged that the general principles and approaches to the archaeological heritage will be contained in a document designed as supplementary planning guidance to the District Local Plan.

Bibliography

Keene DJ 1985 *Survey of Medieval Winchester* Winchester Studies 2, Oxford

English Heritage 1992 *Managing the Urban Archaeological Resource*

RCHME/English Heritage 1993 *Urban Archaeology Databases. Data Standards and Compilers Manual*

Note

All plans are reproduced from Ordnance Survey maps, with the permission of the Controller of Her Majesty's Stationary Office. (c) Crown copyright Reserved. Licence No: LA-08610X.

AN INTRODUCTION TO THE LINCOLN URBAN ARCHAEOLOGICAL DATABASE

Ian George, Lincoln City Council

Lincoln is one of the historic gems of this country with a wealth of rich archaeological deposits beneath its streets. There are presently a number of initiatives taking place that will ensure that its heritage is better managed in the future. This paper will outline the way the management of Lincoln's archaeological heritage is changing in response to the national initiative on urban archaeology.

Lincoln - the city

The city of Lincoln is located on the Witham Gap, a geological break in the limestone escarpment known as the Jurassic ridge or the Lincoln Edge which runs the length of the western part of the county of Lincolnshire. Historically it has developed as a service and market centre for its agricultural hinterland. Heavy engineering industries developed as a spin off from this and remain a major employer today.

The origins of the city lie in the Iron Age. Remains of a late Iron Age round house were discovered close to the Brayford Pool in 1972. Ptolemy in his Geography refers to Lindon as one of two chief tribal centres of the local tribe known as the Coritani (Corieltauvi). Within a few years of the Roman invasion the Ninth Legion Hispana had effected settlement of much of eastern England. A small chain of forts was soon created along the Ermine Street which at Lincoln joined the Fosse Way.

The hill-top fortress at Lincoln is thought to date to the Neronian period (AD54-68). Its fortifications consisted of an earthen bank revetted by timbers and enclosed about 15 hectares (40 acres). When Vespasian resolved to conquer further north and west the Second Legion Adiutrix transferred to Chester and some time between AD85 and 95 *Lindum* became a *colonia*. The legionary defences were retained and a stone face added. The city itself extended down the hill and the defences extended to the river frontage, enclosing an area of 40 hectares. Ribbon development also spread both north and south essentially along the main arterial roads. In the later Roman period Lincoln continued to fair well as it became the capital of the province *Flavia Caesariensis*.

In 313 Constantine I declared Christianity an official religion and Lincoln was represented at a Council of Bishops held at Arles in 314.

Lincoln remained a significant settlement throughout the post-Roman period. The presence of an early Saxon church on the site of the late Roman church and references to Bishop Paulinus visiting Lincoln in 628/9 by Bede indicate the city's ecclesiastical importance. Lincoln was one of the five boroughs of the Danelaw. A site on the corner of Flaxengate and Grantham Street is one of the most extensive excavations undertaken on a site of this period anywhere in the country.

The significance of Lincoln in the mid-11th century is reflected in the construction of a royal castle here by William the Conqueror. The cathedral was consecrated in 1092. The city thrived throughout the medieval period and has a fine stock of medieval buildings. A period of decline followed but Lincoln thrived once more when heavy engineering developed in the mid-19th century.

Planning system

Archaeology is a material consideration in the planning process. This is most clearly stated in Planning Policy Guidance Note 16 'Archaeology and Planning' (PPG16) which was launched in Lincoln in 1990. PPG16 has been successful in raising the status of archaeology not only within planning departments but across the full range of local authority decision making. It has also had a major impact on the type of archaeological work that is being undertaken. In order to offer the best possible advice to those seeking planning permission and to enable the highest quality of management decision to be made accurate information is required.

It was clear from early reaction to the PPG that the historic urban centres were not sufficiently well documented to allow local planning authorities to make an informed decision about the threat to the archaeological resource. Wainwright (1993) outlined the evolving national approach to this issue and concluded that "the management of the urban archaeological resource is an exceptionally challenging and complex task". Here more than anywhere it is critical to not only know where sites and deposits are but to be able to predict where they might be. The main issue is that our historic towns are, on the one hand, the most important archaeological sites in the country but, on the other hand, are areas of dense population and considerable development pressure. Wainwright (1993) stated that effective management of the urban archaeological resource requires frameworks, information, expertise and resources. It is in support of local authorities achieving these objectives that English Heritage is backing and funding Urban Archaeology Databases (UADs) across England.

Lincoln UAD

Lincoln City Council has commissioned the City of Lincoln Archaeology Unit (CLAU) to provide an Urban Archaeology Database. The UAD covers the full extent of the administrative district of Lincoln. The project will result in a series of linked databases and geographic representations of the data. UADs are fundamentally different from a county SMR (the established planning databases) in that they normally consist of three parallel databases and computerised mapping.

The first is referred to as 'Sites' and takes the form of a record of all the recognition events that have taken place in the city. These events range from finds of individual artefacts to observations like watching briefs through to full excavations. A recognition event can also be the depiction of a monument in a picture or on a map. The second is known as the 'Monuments' database and consists of the archaeological features that can be interpreted from the recognition events. The separation of these two elements is the fundamental structural difference between the UADs and existing SMRs. Within the UAD, the relationship between the two databases, Sites and Monuments, is complex. For example, various excavations on the one monument of the Roman forum will lead to the creation of one record for that monument. On the other hand, one large excavation may reveal elements of several monuments from several periods. The third element comes from the depth data available from the excavated sites and is known as the 'Deposit model'. When mapped these data will indicate the height above sea level at which five important levels occur across the city. The deposit model will produce a contour map of the ancient ground levels represented by the top of natural, top of Roman, top of Anglo-Saxon, top of late Medieval as well as the modern ground surface. These three databases are linked to a fourth which is a record of the sources (mainly bibliographic) used to create the other three records.

The Lincoln UAD has evolved out of the work currently being undertaken by CLAU on the English Heritage funded Post-Excavation Project. Many of the recognition events recorded in the Sites database have been undertaken by CLAU. Others have come from antiquarian reports, early maps and museum records. Specific tasks of data collection have also been undertaken within the UAD project to record historic buildings, areas of housing with cellars and topographical detail.

It is of fundamental importance that accurate mapping of recorded elements is available. Initial development of the system has been done on a Geographic Information System developed by Dominic Powlesland of the West Heslerton Project and known as G-Sys and on Cartology (FastCad GIS). Digital data have been designed to be exportable to other systems which may be used in the future. Both historical and management data are mapped. There are overlays for planning constraints like scheduled ancient monuments, listed buildings and conservation areas. It is also possible to import digitised site plans on to maps and to mark the site of smaller recognition events. There are also plans of the various monuments from the cathedral and Roman defences through to domestic buildings. Each can be displayed as an overlay on the Ordnance Survey map base at any scale and can be related to any planning issue. Together with the mapped deposit model it will become easier to predict the presence and likely quality of deposits in the vicinity of development proposals.

Using the UAD

Following the construction of the databases the project will move into an assessment phase. In Lincoln the Urban Archaeology Assessment is to be produced jointly with the Post-Excavation Publication Project and will be published as a statement of our current knowledge and understanding of the history and archaeology of the city. This will then be followed by the development of an Urban Archaeological Strategy from which, it is anticipated, will be developed Supplementary Planning Guidance. This will give the known archaeological resource of the city a statutory status within a land-use planning system which is increasingly development plan led.

The City Council is responsible for the management of several of the city's ancient monuments - including Newport Arch, the Stonebow, St Mary's Guildhall and Jew's House. Recording of maintenance works carried out on these monuments can be held within the UAD and the system can then be used to trigger future conservation works.

Linked to the above is the need to promote these monuments. The database can feed into the tourism activities of the city council and help to increase the information made available to the public - both visitors and residents.

Conclusion

As part of the national initiative on urban archaeology Lincoln City Council has commissioned the production of an Urban Archaeology Database. The city council will use this as the basis for the production of a policy framework for the management and promotion of the city's heritage. This will consist of positive and proactive management and will see the creation of greater links between those who are responsible for the management and promotion of the city's heritage.

Acknowledgements

For their helpful comments on the draft of this published paper I am grateful to Keith Laidler, Director of Planning, Lincoln City Council and Mick Jones, The Director, City of Lincoln Archaeology Unit. The paper was originally presented by Paul Miles, formerly of the City of Lincoln Archaeology Unit.

References

Dept of the Environment 1990 *Planning Policy Guidance Note 16: Archaeology and Planning* (PPG16)

Jones, M J 1988 Lincoln, in Webster G (ed) *Fortress into City* 145-166

Jones, M J 1993 The latter days of Roman Lincoln, in Vince A (ed) *Pre-Viking Lindsey* 14-28, Lincoln Archaeological Studies No.1

Vince, A G and Jones, M J 1990 *Lincoln's Buried Archaeological Heritage* Lincoln

Wainwright, G J 1993 The management of change: archaeology and planning *Antiquity* 67, 416-421

PLYMOUTH'S URBAN ARCHAEOLOGICAL DATABASE AND DEPOSIT MODEL

Keith Ray and Sarah Noble, Plymouth City Council

The implementation of the Urban Archaeological Database (UAD) project in Plymouth forms part of the national programme initiated by English Heritage, which has been developed as a means of documenting, assessing and managing the surviving archaeology of England's historic towns. Jointly funded by Plymouth City Council and by English Heritage, the project was carried out from early June 1995 until January 1997. Due to the relatively small scale of the task of UAD compilation in Plymouth, a pilot study was not undertaken in advance of the full project, which was initially designed to run over a nine and a half month period.

With the increasing volumes of archaeological investigation undertaken since the introduction of PPG 16 in 1990, it had become apparent that the successful management and conservation of this resource is dependent upon the availability of relevant, accessible data. This has lead English Heritage to promote a nationwide programme, which will result in the production of individual management policies for the archaeology of those historic towns involved. For each of these thirty or so towns, a three phase project will be undertaken to develop a management strategy. After the creation of an Urban Archaeological Database (UAD), designed as a computerised index to the major sources of archaeological information, an Urban Archaeological Assessment (UAA) will be produced, to determine the importance of the known resource within the local, regional and national context and potentially to discuss an appropriate research agenda for each town. Informed by the UAA, an Urban Archaeological Strategy (UAS), will identify the likely pressures from future development and identify means of minimising further loss of the archaeological resource.

THE ARCHAEOLOGICAL RESOURCE IN PLYMOUTH

Prehistoric and Roman
Evidence for prehistoric and Roman activity has been recovered from several locations within the UAD area, although development from these periods has yet to be defined. The existence of a settlement from the late Bronze Age across the Sound from Sutton Harbour (Cunliffe 1988), the retrieval of a Bronze Age palstave during excavations at Vauxhall Street in 1990 (Exeter Archaeology, site archive No 434), and observations made in the late 19th century, indicate some potential for earlier phases of occupation. Evidence for Roman activity includes findspots of Roman coins, a possible Romano-British burial uncovered in Stillman Street in the 19th century (Worth 1890, 7-8) and extensive tile deposits encountered during the Woolster Street excavations in the 1960s (Barber 1986, 11). As the Roman mean shoreline is presumed to have been lower than today, it is possible that structures may survive within what later became the harbour.

Medieval
The estate of Sutton is recorded in the Domesday Book as being held by the King and the site of the manor of Sutton (later Sutton Valletort) is believed to be near the 12th century parish church of St Andrew. It has not been traced archaeologically, although excavations to the south of the church in the mid 1970s recorded features possibly dated to the 13th century (Fairclough 1979). It appears that the town developed around two areas; Sutton Prior, on the western arm of Sutton Pool, was granted to the Priors of Plympton and became the urban area, while Sutton Valletort (later Old Town), on the higher ground westwards, around St Andrews Church and along Old Town Street to the north, was held by the Valletort family (Gill 1993, 21ff). No extensive below ground archaeological observations have been made in the area of Sutton Valletort and redevelopment in the 19th and 20th centuries has limited the opportunities for tracing the nature of any early settlement here. No material dating from earlier than the 13th century (from the medieval development of the settlement) has yet been recovered from the waterfront locations (in Sutton Prior) investigated, but there is potential for gaining information about the early fishing settlement here which may have formed the nucleus of the port town (Ray 1995, 60).

Rapid growth of the port followed the granting of market rights to the Priors in the late 13th century and late 13th/early 14th century saw the development of

32

Plymouth into a major trading and naval port (Fair-clough 1979, 7). Excavations around the western arm of the harbour have confirmed that the structures and reclamation deposits associated with this continuing development of the harbour and its facilities probably represent the most important surviving archaeological deposits, in terms of volume and quality, within the city. At the Woolster Street site, a series of excavations carried out in the 1960s recorded a complex sequence of waterfront development dating from the 13th to the 18th centuries (Barber 1986). More recently, an evaluation at 130 Vauxhall Street in 1994 (Stead and Rance 1995) encountered substantial waterlogged deposits predating the medieval reclamation and then a sequence of reclamation from at least the 15th century. In late 1996, excavations at the Parade revealed a deeply stratified sequence of deposits over six metres deep, which clarified the nature of the development in this part of Sutton Harbour and produced evidence of varied human activity in the vicinity (Bedford 1997). The survival of deposits in other locations is highly variable, although the 1989 excavation of medieval tenements at Vauxhall Street (Henderson and Knight 1991) demonstrated the considerable potential of sites even with shallow and partly truncated stratigraphy.

Other monuments in the town have been identified and

vestigations on the site of the castle in the late 1950s and early 1960s located neither remains of the castle itself nor any contemporary structures. The evidence indicated that soon after the castle had been demolished in the late 17th century, the area had been quarried and subsequently used as a communal rubbish dump (Barber 1979a, 1). The site and form of the medieval castle is known solely from cartographic evidence and other depictions. Documentary research has been used to identify the location of the Franciscan friary (Barber 1973) and to counter the long-held belief that the town was walled in the medieval period (although it is possible that the town may have been enclosed by earthwork defences; Barber 1979b). The locations of at least two possible earlier guild buildings have also been suggested (Ray 1995, 70-71).

Post-medieval
Investigation into the Civil War siege works has taken place at several locations since the western side of Charles Fort was recorded in 1976. Excavations on the site of Maidenhead Fort in 1991 and the presumed site of Terrour Fort in 1992 did not recover any evidence in these locations. However, investigations between 1992 and 1994 established that the limestone and shale wall of Resolution Fort (Fig 1), at the north-east extremity

Fig 1 Resolution Fort (bastion of Plymouth's Civil War defensive wall) under excavation in 1992, looking north

in many cases located (although very little has been examined archaeologically) and the locations of the town's major markets, the later Corporation guildhall, the medieval castle and the Carmelite friary are known. Of these, however, only part of the precinct of the latter has been excavated (Henderson 1995). A series of in-

of the line of the inner siege defences, survived to a height of about one metre, with a three and a half metre wide external rock-cut ditch. Although the alignment of the western part of the walled circuit is still unknown, sufficient archaeological and cartographic evidence has

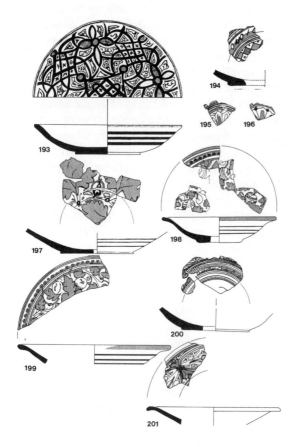

Fig 2 16th-17th century Italian Montelupo ware vessels from the Castle Street excavations

been assembled to determine the eastern part of the circuit reasonably accurately (Henderson 1995).

Rapid economic growth during the Commonwealth prompted substantial development of the harbour side along the northern and eastern shores of Sutton Harbour. Some investigation of these areas has been carried out, and at Hawkers Avenue in 1994 the development of the waterfront was traced from 1650 onwards, including the substantial remains of two merchants houses and warehouses (Stead and Watts 1997). Excavations and fabric recording at the mid 17th century Chinahouse warehouse took place in 1990 (Egan 1990) and subsequent investigations on an adjacent site, Shepherd's Wharf, recorded the contemporary Rattenbury's Great House (Pye and Stead 1994; Stead 1997). Of particular significance is the extensive range of imported products which survive in the material record, representing the town's trading contacts with a wide range of overseas partners. This has been seen at many of the sites excavated in the town, but of particular note in this respect are the Castle Street excavations carried out in the late 1950s and the 1960s already discussed (Barber 1986)(Fig 2).

The development of conservation archaeology in Plymouth

Archaeological recording has been carried out in Plymouth since the late 1950s. Until the late 1980s it had been confined to several large-scale archaeological excavations, the salvage recording of a small number of buildings, and a range of opportunistic observations made during demolition or construction projects. In the late 1980s, a more formalised approach to the archaeological resource was introduced, with advice on the archaeological significance of potential development sites being provided by Devon County Council staff.

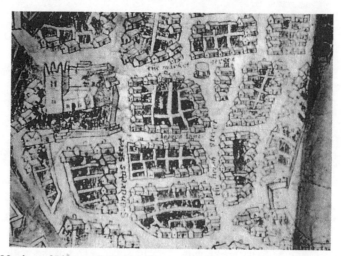

Fig 3 Extract from c.1592 plan of Plymouth (Untitled, attr. R Adams), showing St Andrew's Church, the market cross and part of the waterfront (Hatfield CPM I 35: Skelton and Summerson Catalogue no 25)

Prior to the full implementation of PPG 16 here in 1992, when a City Archaeological Officer was appointed, many potentially important and complex sites were developed without record. Although the small-scale opportunistic observations, often limited to individual photographs, make a useful contribution to the overall picture of the city's historic development, they do not constitute a full record of the archaeological deposits removed and the historic buildings demolished, and prior to the UAD Project, none of these records had been systematically examined. The enormous upturn in the volume of archaeological investigations being carried out as a consequence of planning conditions since 1992 has substantially increased the archaeological information available for the town. Many detailed records that are more consistent and are produced to a higher standard than previously have now been created.

Additional UAD data sources
The variable quality and limited extent of the early recording has necessitated a wide ranging approach to the other available sources of data during UAD creation. Use has been made of cartographic evidence (Fig 3), the strong naval heritage of the city being reflected in the many maps produced. In addition to determining the location and developmental history of key monuments, they do in some cases give an indication of the ground plan and occasionally the form of built structures. In total, twenty-six maps have been included in

the UAD as recognition events, the earliest of which dates from 1539-45 and the latest of which dates from 1831.

The photographic collections held by Plymouth City Museum and Art Gallery (PCMAG) have also been consulted, as many include images of medieval and later buildings since removed, and are the sole record of many of these important structures. The most useful have been the late 19th century Rugg-Monk collection (Fig 4), the City Engineers' record of post-war engineering works and the Goodridge Collection.

DATA INPUT, STORAGE AND RETRIEVAL

Data structure
The data structure employed for the database is based on *Urban Archaeological Databases: Data Standards and Compilers Manual* (English Heritage and RCHM(E)). The overall structure is derived directly from this advisory document and any differences are limited to points of detail. Fundamental to the structure of the database is the distinction drawn between 'sites' and 'monuments', and the role played by archaeological elements in providing the link between them.

Recognition events
A 'site' in this context is defined as a recognition event and derives from any observation of archaeological

Fig 4 A view of Palace Court (a 17th century and earlier merchant's house complex) during demolition in the late 19th century (Plymouth City Museum: PCMAG Rugg Monk series, AR.50.59.73)

information. Each episode of observation, or recognition event, is given a separate record in the database, noting summary information, while the location is plotted on the GIS. As mentioned above, a below ground observation, an historic photograph, a cartographic depiction or documentary research each represents an example of a potential recognition event. Each may record one or more archaeological elements, and occasionally none at all, and more than one recognition event may relate to a single location.

Archaeological elements
An archaeological element comprises a component of the archaeological resource identified through a recognition event. The identification of these components forms the basic interpretation of the resource, potentially contributing to the interpretation of a monument. The types of elements defined range from the simple (eg wall), to the complex (eg merchants' house), as the definition of an element is determined by the ability to interpret a feature. The terms used to define the archaeological elements have largely been drawn from the Thesaurus of Monument Types (RCHME and English Heritage), although several extra terms which have been identified will be submitted for inclusion in the Thesaurus. The archaeological elements for each recognition event listed within the database are referenced directly to the monuments of which they are components (where relevant).

Monuments
A monument is a structure identified within the historic core, which is judged to be of sufficient archaeological and/or historic significance to warrant inclusion. In Plymouth, this includes buildings, fortifications and structures associated with the historic waterfront. A monument may be as complex as the precinct of one of the friaries, or as simple as an individual quay structure. Any recognition event may only record part of a given monument and several recognition events may combine to provide all the known information about a monument. The separate definition of recognition events as distinct from the monuments themselves is intended to ensure that the evidence for a monument is differentiated from interpretation and discussion.

The study area
The study area covers a total of 4.2 km^2, which is sufficient to include both the historic core of the city and, for example, defensive outworks. The extent of this area has been determined by the non-archaeological criteria of the national grid. The area outside the UAD study area will be covered by the new Sites and Monuments Record for Plymouth. Database records have now been created for nearly 500 recognition events and an initial draft of nearly 150 monuments has been produced.

Database and GIS
The UAD in Plymouth has been created within a relational database which functions in tandem with a Geographical Information System (GIS) installed with a digitising pad (Fig 5). The summary information for each recognition event is stored in the relational database, in a structure which allows the user to perform queries on the data and to print out the results as customised reports. Future development of the system is intended to increase the range of data sets available from the database (see below).

The GIS has been used as the base for plotting sets of archaeological data to create a range of 'overlays' (described below), which can be viewed in conjunction with the OS base map and/or each other. The location of each recognition event has been plotted, with an information 'window' attached to each for displaying summary information. The plotted overlay records can also be searched to display and print answers to queries.

The applications in use are Paradox for Windows and GGP for Windows respectively and both are available through the internal IT network set up for environmental planning services. This allows map data to be exported, for printing in colour or to be plotted at a larger scale than is possible on the locally available printers. Using the network, it will also be possible to make any of the overlays available to other departments of the City Council.

At the outset of the project, the DOS version of GGP had been installed. However, GGP for Windows has since been released and this is now in use. In addition to a more user-friendly working environment, a far greater range of functions is now available and the development of this application in a Windows environment is continuing. Further work will be carried out to convert all the UAD map files for use in GGP for Windows.

Mapping
Sites
An overlay has been constructed on which the location of all recognition events has been plotted, each represented by a symbol. The information window gives the record number, the location of the site, the type of

Fig 5 The Paradox-based Urban Archaeological Database during the record compilation process

observation, the date of the observation and the number of archaeological elements (see above) recorded. It uses codes to indicate the date(s) of any features recorded and to differentiate natural features. An additional overlay shows the extents of all located excavations.

Monuments
In addition to an overlay which shows the location of all known monuments, several thematic overlays will be constructed. These will combine data from recognition events with known monuments to reconstruct the locations and where possible the extents of associated features. These will show the leats and conduits system dating from the late 16th century onwards, and the defensive features constructed during the Civil War. A further sequence of overlays forms a predictive deposit model for the waterfront in the vicinity of Sutton Harbour (see below).

Additional overlays
To augment the effectiveness of the data held on the GIS, several other overlays are and will be available. The results of the Barbican Conservation Area Survey (BCAS; see below) have been input into the GIS and can be viewed with the UAD overlays to carry out a rapid assessment of the nature of a site. Several of the overlays cover the whole city, including the extents of the ten Conservation Areas currently designated. In addition, once the Listed Review currently in progress has been completed, an overlay to show the location and

extent of Listed Buildings within the City will be constructed and will be available on the internal network as will be the extents of the Scheduled Ancient Monuments. The locations associated with the records in the new Sites and Monuments Record for Plymouth will be plotted and available on a further overlay.

DEPOSIT MODELLING

Deposit models have been constructed as part of several UAD projects, to map the known and predicted extents and depths of surviving archaeological deposits. This data can be used in advance of development to identify the areas of survival and loss and to predict the nature, extent and volumes of archaeological deposits. The York Development and Archaeology Study, produced as a pilot scheme in 1991, includes a sequence of maps which show projected contours of the ground surface at different successive points in time, areas of known anaerobic deposits and areas where the archaeology has been largely or totally destroyed.

For much of the UAD study area in Plymouth, however, these deep stratigraphic deposits do not exist. The nature of construction in the historic core of the city, whereby subsequent development has generally terraced into the earlier remains, has removed many of the archaeological deposits. In addition, 19th century slum clearances and road widening, social housing and other construction projects in the 1930s, and post-war clearance and redevelopment of the blitzed areas of central Plymouth, have all contributed to the further destruction of the archaeology of the historic core. However, it has been possible to carry out deposit modelling for two distinct but overlapping areas, using very different methodology and mapping display. The Barbican Conservation Area Survey sought to determine the potential survival of significant deposits and fabric. In contrast, the deposit modelling undertaken for Sutton Pool aims to predict the depth and extent, and even period, of the deposits.

Barbican Conservation Area Survey

The Barbican Conservation Area covers part of the historic core of the town, along the western side of Sutton Harbour. Its northern part encompasses the zone which has the highest levels of survival of historic fabric both above and below ground. Despite the significance and extent of the archaeological resource known to survive in this area, no quantification or survey had previously been undertaken to establish survival and potential. Even into the 1980s significant sites and buildings had been developed without record. In view of the continuing development pressures in the area and the potential for loss of archaeological deposits, a survey of the Barbican Conservation Area was carried out early in 1996 (but not formally as part of the UAD project). In order provide an extensive indication of survival, potential and loss, the survey identified the archaeological potential of each plot of land, the condition and probable age of standing buildings and the location of potential development sites. In this way, the current archaeological status of each plot of land across the area has been recorded. The results of this survey have been built into a series of seven overlays for display in the GIS to provide an extensive model of the archaeological potential of the area.

Sutton Harbour deposit model
Reclamation deposits
A more detailed model of the deep reclamation deposits that survive in the vicinity of Sutton Harbour is being constructed. Up to 6m of deposits survive below ground, representing the sequence of waterfront reclamation activity dating from at least circa 1250. As mentioned above, Roman tile has been recovered from the lowest harbour silts in some areas and it is possible that early structures may survive within the harbour. The waterlogged nature of the lower levels result in high preservation of organic remains and environmental material and important groups of artefacts and faunal remains have been retrieved from the deeply stratified

deposits. A variety of sources is being used to construct a deposit model which aims to show the sequence of historic reclamation and associated waterfronts.

Contours on bedrock
The basis of this predictive model is an overlay showing the contours of the surface of bedrock, which has been constructed using data from both archaeological and engineering projects. Although investigative engineering groundworks supply little data from which secure archaeological interpretation may be drawn, the total area investigated archaeologically down to bedrock is very small and of necessity the bulk of the data relating to the height of bedrock has been derived from engineering sources. Relatively little data is available for the western side of Sutton Harbour, as few development projects that would have generated engineering investigations have not taken place here.

Contours of the lower silts
It is also intended to construct a similar surface mapping for the lower silt levels, representing the earliest deposits within the natural harbour, and deriving from sedimentary processes. It is possible to estimate the probable depths of these from some of the borehole logs available, although interpretations of the descriptions of deposits from these logs are inevitably less secure than for a description of bedrock. For certain locations, archaeological and engineering observations overlap, which may enable a comparison of results.

Period overlays
Detail relating to the historical development of the waterfront has been drawn from documentary research undertaken for the archaeological projects that have been carried out in the area. In combination with the archaeological and cartographic evidence, it is being used to create a sequence of period overlays, reconstructing the layout and alignment of structures forming the existing waterfronts. The dates of these reconstructions are at intervals of between 50 and 100 years, corresponding with periods of known expansion, and making use of the evidence available from historic maps, to give sequence of 'point-in-time' depictions of the waterfront. The earliest complete plan which shows the waterfront in any detail is the 1725 Board of Ordnance map, although a Bernard de Gomme map of 1672, centred on the then new Royal Citadel, does show the western arm of Sutton Harbour and part of Cattedown. In combination with the period overlays, more sophisticated predictions can be made about the nature of the resource. As the results of future archaeological projects are incorporated, predictions can be proved and the model further refined.

THE FUTURE

Further development of the database

With the substance of the UAD complete and in use, consideration is being given to the future development of the system. The advantages of using the GIS to display map-based data have proved considerable, particularly in combination with the search and display facilities now available and it is likely that the results of any extensive survey work carried out by the City Council's Archaeology Section in the future will be added to the system. The use of the database will continue to be expanded and the construction of a database listing all reports produced for archaeological recording projects across the whole city is being planned.

Implications for data structure

During the development of the data structure for the UAD programme, it has become apparent that there are implications for the structure of other record systems holding archaeological data, particularly the County based Sites and Monuments Records (SMRs). The separation of records relating to archaeological observations from records relating to the interpretation of monuments in the UAD data structure is the key difference, and a debate is currently underway about the desirability of restructuring SMRs. Once Plymouth becomes a unitary authority in April 1998, the SMR for the city will be held and maintained by the Archaeology Section of Plymouth City Council and this may be an opportunity to develop and implement a new data structure. However, the implementation of a comprehensive revision and restructuring of SMRs nationwide will not be undertaken lightly, as the cost would be considerable. The debate continues.

The next stage

Many sites and buildings of archaeological importance have been lost with little or no record and the full significance of the archaeology of Plymouth has tended, until recently, to be underestimated. This project has systematically examined, evaluated and presented the information currently available for the archaeology of the historic core of Plymouth. It provides an overview and a system of cross-referencing, making the archaeological record more accessible for research and as a tool for use in the planning process. In doing so, it has created an effective tool in the management of the archaeological resource and provided the starting point for the next stage in the process, the Urban Archaeological Assessment.

References

Thesaurus of Monument Types: a standard for use in archaeological and architectural records RCHM(E) and English Heritage

York Development and Archaeology Study Ove Arup and Partners and York University in association with Bernard Thorpe

Barber, James 1979a *Introduction*, in Gaskell Brown, C (ed) 1979, 1-2

Barber, James 1979b New Light on Old Plymouth *Proceedings of the Plymouth Athenaeum* IV, 55-66

Barber, James 1986 *Buildings and Quays*, in Gaskell Brown, C (ed) 1986 11-12

Barber, Jennifer 1973 New light on the Plymouth Friaries *Transactions of the Devonshire Association* 105, 59-73

Bedford, J B 1997 *Plymouth Sewage Treatment Scheme Tunnel Contract Shafts 7 & 13* Archaeological Excavation Interim Summary Report, Exeter Archaeology Report No 97.35

Cunliffe, B 1988 *Mount Batten, Plymouth - A Prehistoric and Roman Port* Oxford University Monograph No 26

Egan, G 1990 Post-medieval Britain in 1989 *Post-medieval Archaeology* 24, 173-6

Fairclough, G J 1979 *Plymouth Excavations: St Andrews Street 1976* Plymouth Museum Archaeological Series, 2

Gaskell Brown, C (ed) 1979 *Plymouth Excavations: Castle Street: The Pottery* Plymouth Museum Archaeological Series, 1

Gaskell Brown, C (ed) 1986 *Plymouth Excavations: The Medieval Waterfront. Woolster Street: The Finds; Castle Street; The Finds* Plymouth Museum Archaeological Series, 3

Gill, C 1993 *Plymouth: a new history* Devon Books
Henderson, C G 1995 Excavations at Plymouth Whitefriars, 1989-1994, in Ray, K 1995 *Archaeological In-*

vestigations and Research in Plymouth, Volume I: 1992-93 Plymouth Archaeology Occasional Publication No 2, 47-58

Knight, M and Henderson, C 1991 Plymouth, Brock House, Vauxhall Street, in Neuk, B S, Margeson, S and Hurley, M Medieval Britain and Ireland in 1991 Medieval Archaeology 35, 217-18

Pye, A R and Stead, P M 1994 Archaeological assessment and field evaluation of Shepherd's Wharf, Coxside, Plymouth Exeter Museums Archaeological Field Unit Report No 94.51

Ray, K 1995 'Sutton-Super-Plymouth': a medieval port, in Ray, K (ed) 1995 Archaeological Investigations in Plymouth, Volume I: 1992-93 Plymouth Archaeology Occasional Publication No 2, 59-81

Stead, P M 1997 Archaeological excavation and recording at Shepherd's Wharf, Coxside, Plymouth, 1996 Exeter Archaeology Report No 97.21

Stead, P M and Rance, C 1995 Archaeological Assessment and Field Evaluation of 130 Vauxhall Street, Sutton Wharf, Plymouth Exeter Museums Archaeological Field Unit Report 95.01

Stead, P M and Watts, M A 1997 Excavations at Hawkers Avenue, North Quay, 1994-95, in Ray, K (ed) forthcoming Archaeological Investigations in Ply-

mouth, Volume II: 1994-95 Plymouth Archaeology Occasional Publication No 4

Worth, R N 1890 History of Plymouth

Unpublished sources:

Noble, S (draft) A survey of archaeological potential and historic fabric in the Barbican Conservation Area

Noble, S 1996 Urban Archaeological Database: User's guide to the Paradox database Plymouth City Council, City Archaeology

Sharif, S and Ray, K (Draft) Archaeology and Development in Plymouth: a catalogue and summary of reports

Urban Archaeological Databases: Data Standards and Compilers Manual English Heritage and RCHM(E)

1994 Plymouth Urban Archaeological Assessment Project: Urban Archaeological Database for Sutton Harbour Urban Core Area. UAD Project Outline (amended version)

1996 Plymouth Urban Archaeological Assessment Project: Urban Archaeological Database for Sutton Harbour Urban Core Area. Phase Two Proposals: UAD, Part Two; UAA Study

ELECTRONIC JOURNALS AND ARCHIVING

Alan Vince, Department of Archaeology, University of York

This paper is divided into three parts. In the first, I describe at some length the archives of the City of Lincoln Archaeology Unit, for whom I worked between 1988 and 1995: first producing an electronic archive of excavations carried out between 1972 and 1987 and then being part of a team involved in the analysis and publication of those excavations. In the second part, I look at the way in which *Internet Archaeology*, the electronic journal for archaeology of which I am the Managing Editor, has dealt with the division between publication and archive. Finally, in the third part of the paper, I re-examine the division of archaeological fieldwork and research into published and unpublished material and indulge in some futurology, looking forward to a world in which museums, excavation units, researchers and academic publications are fully computerised.

Part One: The Lincoln Electronic Archaeological Archive

The electronic archive of the City of Lincoln Archaeology Unit can be divided into two clear parts. These correspond to the Site Archive and Research Archive as defined in English Heritage's *Management of Archaeological Projects (2nd Edn)* which, in line with current usage, I refer to throughout as MAP2. I should point out, though, that this division is perhaps clearer in the case of past excavations in Lincoln than it will be in future since in 1988 we were faced, essentially, with records created on paper, drawing film and photographic emulsion (and the physical finds and samples removed from the site). Computers were not regularly used except as word processors. This statement should not belittle the work of Kev Camidge, who did much experimental computer recording and analytical work using Lincoln excavation data, but whose methods were not followed through. This clear split is obviously less easy to maintain when the post-excavation work on an archaeological site starts with a computerised site archive.

Site Records

Lincoln excavations were recorded either using notebooks or some sort of record sheet or card pre-printed with field names. These formal records, made to serve as a permanent record of the excavation, are supplemented by formal measured plans, sections and elevations and by informal sketches and notes. The latter are actually the most revealing documents since they show why an excavation proceeded along certain lines and where the excavators laboured under misapprehensions. As a first stage in creating the electronic archive computerised indices were created of all paper records and certain records were then transcribed, in all or part, onto computer. Stratigraphic records and finds registers were checked as they were transcribed, so that the final archive was not simply an unintelligent copy of the paper record but a database in which one could have some confidence in the quality of the data (although, obviously, it still depended on the quality of the original excavation and post-excavation procedures).

The Research Archive

The research archive was created directly onto computer, or with the use of temporary recording sheets. It consisted of a database recording the phasing and interpretation of every recorded deposit and an on-line description of each context group together with identifications and quantification of artefacts and ecofacts from the excavations. The research archive also consists of data of two levels. Firstly, there were records whose prime purpose was to enable the potential of the material for further study to be determined and secondly there were records whose prime purpose was to allow inferences about activity on the site itself to be made. These inferences might be chronological, pertaining to site formation, or of more general application. The important point is that the perceived purpose of the record affected the care with which it was created and the design and relationships of the data table. As with the site archive, however, the initial distinction between the two types of research archive record could not really be sustained. In certain cases, for example, the amount of work required to demonstrate that a class of finds was worthy of further study was no less than that required to make the permanent record and in many others the amount of disputed work (ie the discrepancy between the effort required to produce the "full" record and that required to "assess" the potential value of making that record) was very low.

Furthermore, as work on the Lincoln electronic archive progressed, it became clearer and clearer that post-excavation work, as developed at Lincoln, was not linear. Work on pottery and other finds, animal bone assemblages, botanical samples and so on was constantly producing results which led to a better understanding of the site stratigraphy. The model which we had followed, site recording; initial post-excavation; analysis; research and publication, was simply not suited to the work we were doing. Nor could we modify our methods to make them fit this linear model.

To give an example, we could take a site where, through analysis of the excavation records and the recovered finds, we could assign each element of the site stratigraphy both a value on the scale of reliability of excavation and a value based on the likelihood of the artefacts within it being contemporary with the deposit (ie a residuality index). Presenting dating evidence as a simple list of "latest finds" from the deposits would clearly be misleading without reference to these other factors. On the other hand, presenting all the datable artefacts (or even worse all the artefacts/ecofacts whose presence/absence might affect the likely date or phase of a deposit) would clearly be impossible in a printed publication. Furthermore, as research progressed so various working hypotheses failed and had to be replaced: type X might be earlier rather than later than type Y; type Z might actually be divisible into two types Za and Zb of differing date or interpretation.

What seemed to be required, therefore, was the means to publish a provisional statement about an excavation's date and interpretation with the ability to keep on collecting information about that site's stratigraphy and associated finds. Periodically, it would be necessary to re-examine this statement and perhaps replace it with a revised one.

Whilst the Lincoln post-excavation work was probably one of the most extreme instances yet tackled of trying to integrate the results of a large number of interventions I do not think that this means that conclusions based on our experience are invalid. If anything, perhaps, problems were raised on our project which have not yet become evident on many other sites. After all, most archaeological publication has to take place in a virtual vacuum since there are not the frameworks in place required to integrate the results of different pieces of fieldwork.

To summarise, therefore, I think that the Lincoln post-excavation project demonstrated that it is necessary to make arrangements for the continued study of the site records: both the site archive and research archive. It also suggested that the conceptual difference between the various types of archive may be real but is bound to be blurred. In any case, the entire archive - whether recorded on site or off and whether recorded for particular purposes or for posterity - needs to be maintained as a working system. It is at this point that I want to describe some of the work carried out for *Internet Archaeology* and to extrapolate from these two examples to what we could do in the future.

Part Two: Internet Archaeology

Internet Archaeology is an electronic journal which resides on the World Wide Web. It is by no means the first example of the use of the Internet to publish archaeological research but is the first, probably, which has attempted to use the Internet as a permanent medium for the publication of that research. A comparison might be between pre-prints and magazine articles - which constitute "grey" literature - and journals of record. The audience for the former consists of fellow workers and interested laymen whilst the audience for the latter may not yet be born. As with all such artificial constructs the boundaries are fuzzy. Seminal work can be published in obscure, hard-to-obtain media whilst our journals are bound to contain some work of no lasting value. Nevertheless, the distinction is important since it affects the way in which information is presented and the choice of information to include.

The first issue of *Internet Archaeology* was published on the Web in September 1996 and contained papers on a variety of subjects. Two of these papers were concerned with methodology: the potential of Virtual Reality Markup Language for archaeology and the use of high-resolution magnetometry in site excavation. The remainder were all based on the study of the results of archaeological excavations and the artefacts found on them.

Firstly, Paul Tyers published a survey of amphoras from Roman Britain (http://intarch.ac.uk/journal/issue1/tyers/index.html). This work followed on from the pioneer work of David Peacock and David Williams and took their work further by being able to plot the find-spots of amphoras throughout Britain and in several cases elsewhere in the Western Empire and then to draw conclusions about the trade which resulted in these distribution patterns. Unlike a printed publication, it is possible both to look at the published distribution maps and to find out more about them. By clicking a mouse on the maps it is possible first to get a larger, more detailed map and then to obtain information on the findspots themselves.

Since this is one of the first works of its kind, it is not possible to go further but clearly a dedicated researcher would want to be able to look at a map, get a list of the findspots and then look at online publications for each one. Questions might include:

- Who identified the amphora sherds?
- How many were there?
- What proportion of the total pottery from the site did they form?
- What was the dating evidence for their context?
- What was thought to be the interpretation of the site where they were found (port, civitas capital, fortress, walled town, unwalled town, princely residence and so on)?

Looked at from the point of view of a single excavation report, papers like this could cut out a tremendous amount of background information which today would have to be repeated, on the assumption that the report would be unintelligible without this data. Looked at from the viewpoint of a museum, one would want to be able to access this report from the museum's own electronic records and to be able to update the report in the light of future research. Most museums keep copies of publications which include artefacts from their collections and in many cases you will find valuable annotations in these copies. Perhaps other specialists have queried the identification, or have had scientific analysis undertaken which confirms it. Graffiti or painted inscriptions may have been recognised or stamps identified and classified. The vessel may be included in an exhibition, or published in a museum's catalogue. At present, a researcher could only access such additional information by writing to each museum in turn (probably to be told that the financial situation being what it is there was no possibility of answering the query).

The second paper to look at is by Allan Peacey and concerns the results of a study that Dr Peacey undertook of the archaeological evidence for the manufacture of clay tobacco pipes. This work involved the study and interpretation of excavation plans and the classification and quantification of pipe-making waste. This material is very disparate. Being post-medieval, it is only in recent times that it has been accepted without question that it belongs in a museum. A number of the collections that Dr Peacey studies are, in consequence, in private hands. Dr Peacey has used his own fabric classification

based on the preparation of the clay rather than the source of the raw materials. He has devised and applied a classification for all the bits of kiln furniture and "furniture supplements" (ie bits of clay utilised during the loading process rather than being pre-formed, fired and reused). This is a good example of a specialised classification which would quite likely cut across the systems employed by the bodies responsible for the post-excavation analysis or curation of the collections. Here too, it has been possible to plot the distribution of different types of evidence and to retrieve this information by findspot, based on the use of clickable maps. At various points, this paper too ought to point back to other published or archive material. There is no consideration of the co-location of other industrial evidence, for example, nor is there any possibility of studying the topography of these production sites in the period immediately prior to the foundation of the pipe manufactory or to examine the loss of coins or use of ceramics on manufacturing sites. To make these studies you need access to a fuller excavation record, as you also would in order to check Dr Peacey's conclusions. In a few cases we know from the text that the plans and interpretations included in this paper are not those of the original excavator. This is, of course, not surprising since most excavators will have come upon only one pipe kiln in their entire excavating careers. They would be most unlikely to have known how one worked and, therefore, to have correctly interpreted all the evidence.

Finally, we come to the paper by Phillipa Tomlinson and Allan Hall on the archaeological evidence for food plants in the British Isles. This paper, to my mind, shows exactly how online publication can work well. The paper is in three parts. The first is a rehearsal of the type of evidence found and the factors affecting its survival and interpretation. The second part, the main body of the paper, is a survey of plant use through time illustrated by summary tables showing the number of deposits of each major period with evidence for the use of a particular foodplant. Part three is a summary of trends in the data and a comparison of the archaeological evidence with that derived from documentary sources.

Except for the most common foodplants, every statement in the second part of this paper could, and should, be hedged around with qualifying statements about the variable quality of the excavations, the poor dating of many archaeobotanical samples, and the exact nature of the evidence. A single seed, for example, is much less convincing evidence for the use of a plant than a deposit containing several hundred seeds. Such an approach would have been tedious in the extreme to read. The alternative, with a printed paper, is to rely on your judgement of the capability of the writer to have made all of these decisions for you or to expand the paper into a monograph accompanied by a mass of tables containing the detail. However, in this case we are able to have a complete database of published archaeobotanical samples from the year dot to 1992, the ArchaeoBotanical Computer Database (or ABCD), sitting in the background waiting to serve up precisely this data. If you want to know all the sites from which apple remains have been recorded it will tell you. It is then possible to go further into the database and see a summary of the stratigraphic details of each sample; a list of all the taxa from those samples and so on.

The ABCD too is a specialist database but, unlike that for clay pipe kilns, it is one with a very wide application. The database allows the authors to record all the nuances of identification beloved by plant taxonomists. It is, in its present form, what is know as metadata - data about data - but there is little in the average archaeobotanist's published data which is not present in the ABCD. In other words, if everyone had guaranteed access to an online copy of the ABCD there would be little justification in publishing one's data in any other format. Furthermore, since the ABCD was constructed to make sense of data of widely varying quality, there is no reason why the same structure could not be used for every situation: from the rapid assessment through to the most detailed study.

Future issues of *Internet Archaeology* will include papers which take these methods of blurring the distinction between data and report into the area of excavation reports, field surveys and the analysis of metal artefacts, as well as continuing with the publication of applications of new technologies to archaeology.

Part Three: The Future
Integrating my conclusions on the shape of archaeological excavation archives based on the Lincoln post-excavation project and electronic publication based on *Internet Archaeology* one comes up with some interesting conclusions. The first question that arises is what ought to happen to a paper, such as those by Drs Tyers, Peacey, Tomlinson and Hall, when new data becomes available. What happens with a print publication is that eventually the author, or another author, will produce a new survey, sometimes merely adding new data and sometimes re-examining or augmenting the previous data. Every year, for example, the Journal of Roman Pottery Studies publishes an index of pottery reports publishing in the preceding year together with keywords indicating the pottery types present in that report.

Once in a while new clay pipe kilns turn up and, most likely, Dr Peacey will be on hand to study them. As we speak, *Historic Scotland* is funding the Environmental Archaeology Unit at York University to augment their ABCD records for Scotland. Will this data appear in *Internet Archaeology*? and, if so, in what form?

There seems to be widespread agreement that the value of the databases accompanying these papers, and their future companions, will be enhanced by their being kept up-to-date. However, if the original paper's data is simply updated it would no longer be possible to maintain the connection between text and data. The text might say that a particular amphora type is unknown before the 4th century whilst the accompanying distribution map could include new 3rd-century examples. The user needs to know what data were considered by the authors so as to evaluate the use those authors made of the data. The solution seems to be to publish supplements to the data, so that it is possible to have an extra box to click in each case stating something like "For data collected between 1996 and 1999 click here". These supplements ought to be accompanied by papers by their authors assessing the value of this new data, referring back to their original papers and either patting themselves on the backs or admitting that new data had led to new interpretations.

Now, in each of the examples given from the current issue of *Internet Archaeology*, a good case can be made for this data living in the journal. The databases are either clearly individual specialists' working tools (as with the clay pipes and amphora papers) or cut across any possible national interests (the ABCD already covers Ireland as well as England, Scotland and Wales). What happens, however, when we come to publish a report on a major archaeological excavation? As I indicated when talking about the Lincoln archive it is clear that such excavation archives will have, eventually, to be living databases to which data added by curators and future specialists and students will be linked. Where should such archives be lodged and whose responsibility should it be to maintain them? These questions are, of course, as much a matter of politics as of logic and pragmatism. They lead on the major problem which has arisen in recent years. Archaeological data, with the advent of PPG16 and commercial archaeology, has suddenly acquired a value. Furthermore, it is more or less agreed that certain classes of data must be maintained for the public good. These include the Sites and Monuments Records, the Urban Archaeology Databases and certain national databases being maintained by the Royal Commissions, English Heritage and the like. Electronic archaeological archives could be seen as the next level of detail down from the SMRs and UADs. Even at Lincoln, where the UAD was created by the same organisation as created the electronic archaeological archive, it was clear that integrating the two would create problems in terms of access and responsibility. Put briefly, in a situation where prior knowledge is a commercial advantage there is little impetus to place information in the public domain and yet much of this prior knowledge was gained through publicly funded research. In the universities there is perhaps less desire to hoard information. Most university-based projects are finite, even if they last for a decade or two, so there is perhaps more acceptance that the data should be placed in the public domain. I therefore predict that the model for future archaeological archives will be formed in the higher education sector and perhaps from there be adopted by museums and local authorities.

I would suggest that one model would be for an archaeological repository (ie a MGC-approved museum) to subcontract its electronic data storage to an external data bank and for journals like *Internet Archaeology* to make links to this data bank. Once data had been handed across to a museum responsibility for its maintenance is passed across to the museum as well and it would be for the museum, or its chosen subcontractors, to keep the data up to date and to control access. In the case of our *Internet Archaeology* papers I would expect the break between the journal's responsibility and that of the museum to be easily definable, using the MDA standards as a guide.

PRESERVATION AND DISPLAY OF ARCHAEOLOGICAL SITES IN NORFOLK: RECENT WORK INVOLVING NORFOLK MUSEUMS SERVICE

John A Davies, Department of Archaeology, Norwich Castle Museum

The involvement of museums and archaeologists in the managing of sites and monuments in the landscape in order to make them accessible and intelligible to the public has generated debate during the 1980s and 90s. An increasing awareness of the necessity to involve the public has stimulated greater partcipation by museums in open site management. There are many issues to be confronted in this area of involvement. These include the initial acquisition of sites, management issues, how sites should be interpreted and explained to the public and how information should be presented on the ground. In Norfolk, since the 1980s, several archaeologically sensitive sites have been acquired by bodies concerned with their protection and preservation. Staff of the Norfolk Museums Service have been involved with these initiatives in recent years.

Archaeologists in Norfolk are employed within three sections of the Norfolk Museums Service. The Norfolk Archaeological Unit is the contracting wing of the organisation which undertakes excavation and fieldwork. Norfolk Landscape Archaeology staff deal with developer and planning issues. The Archaeology Department at Norwich Castle Museum has a curatorial role over the county archaeological collections. As a consequence, there is a wide range of archaeological expertise available across the Service which has been used to assist in the recent programmes of site preservation and presentation. This paper will explain the background and progress to date with some of these major projects and relate the involvement of Norfolk Museums Service staff in these initiatives.

Background to the current situation

Prior to the current situation of protecting archaeological sites in Norfolk, there was a long history of countryside conservation in the county, making use of purchase as a mechanism for protecting endangered areas (Wade-Martins 1996). As long ago as 1926 the Norfolk Naturalists' Trust became the first such county trust to be formed and it now owns, or manages, thirty-eight nature reserves, covering nearly 7000 acres within the county. Also in 1926, the Norfolk Archaeological Trust was created, as a subsidiary group within the Norfolk Archaeological Society. Its original purpose was to protect, through acquisition, selected local historic buildings. It now owns properties in Norwich and Kings Lynn.

In recent years, the Archaeological Trust has become more widely active in the county and its role has developed to include the protection of sites, as well as buildings, through their acquisition, when suitable opportunities arise. The reason behind this development in its role was basically that of an initiative to protect archaeological sites by stopping plough and other physical damage and to improve public access.

The first problem to be overcome when embarking on a policy of site acquisition is that it is very expensive. The method of acquiring finance in Norfolk has varied from site to site but has involved a package in each case, which has included grants from a number of bodies, including English Heritage, local authorities and the Countryside Commission.

Conservation through purchase has now been achieved at several sites in Norfolk. In 1984 the National Trust bought the Saxon Shore fort at Brancaster, on the northwest coast. That site has subsequently been put down to grass. Then, in 1990, it purchased a small motte and bailey castle at Denton, in south-east Norfolk. Over the last five years, the Norfolk Archaeological Trust has acquired three archaeological sites, at Caistor St Edmund, Burgh Castle and Tasburgh. Norfolk Museums Service staff have had most involvement with the Roman sites of Caistor St Edmund and Burgh Castle and it is these which will be looked at in some detail here, in order to communicate Norfolk's efforts to bridge the gap between conventional museums and sites; in effect creating museums in the landscape.

Caistor St Edmund

Background to the site

The Roman town of Caistor St Edmund lies three miles to the south of Norwich. It used to be more widely known and referred to as Caistor-by-Norwich. It was the major Roman regional administrative town, or civitas capital, in northern East Anglia. The site is still visually impressive (Fig 1) with a surviving late Roman flint wall, enclosing some 35 acres, which still stands to a height of 6 metres in the north. The intra-mural area has been levelled but, apart from a Norman church situated in the south-east corner, has not been built on or occupied since the Roman period - in common with the Roman towns of Wroxeter and Silchester. In fact Caistor Roman town is even better preserved than either of those two cases because it has undergone much less excavation. This site is a magnificent resource for future study and has to be preserved to ensure that this is possible for future generations. It is one of our most important national Roman sites in this respect.

'Countryside Stewardship Scheme', to protect the archaeology from further plough damage. This now embraces the defended centre of the town, extensive areas of the suburbs and the amphitheatre to the south.

The acquisition package was complex, involving the support of several separate organisations. English Heritage grant-aided consolidation work on the defensive walls and provided fencing. The Countryside Commission supported public access works. South Norfolk District Council and Norfolk County Council also helped with land acquisition and public access. Shell UK funded the interpretation panels. The National Rivers Authority contributed two footbridges over the riverside walk. Clearance work was carried out by the

Fig 1 Caistor St Edmund, Norfolk. Aerial view of the walled area from the south-west, showing the Roman street layout, defined by parch marks. Photo: Derek A Edwards, Norfolk Air Photographs Library, Norfolk Museums Service)

Involvement of the Norfolk Archaeological Trust
In 1983 the landowner, Mrs Edith Hawkins, died and left as a bequest to the Norfolk Archaeological Trust the core area of the Roman town, as defined by the late Roman walls. The bequest did not include any of the extra-mural town and it was evident that if the town was to be properly protected, more would need to be done. Accordingly, the Trust set out to purchase more of the town and its setting, including the ditch beyond the walls, the extra-mural streets and suburban areas. The Trust now owns the whole block of land between the River Tas in the west and the Norwich road in the east, encompassing 120 acres. All of the land has been put down to grass as part of the Countryside Commission's

British Trust for Conservation Volunteers.

Having acquired the site, the Trust's main intention then became threefold. They needed to protect the site and its setting for posterity. They wanted to open, and to interpret, the site for the public. In all of these areas, expertise of the local archaeologists has been called upon.

The presentation of the archaeological site within its setting was a principal objective. It was considered imperative that this initiative be seen as more than just an exercise to protect the archaeology. The preservation of the site within its landscape and natural setting were also fundamental requirements. To this end, natural habitats across the site have been encouraged and restored, within which wildlife and flora can flourish.

Archaeological work on the site
Initial work on the site to prepare it for opening to the public allowed for some limited archaeological investigation by the Norfolk Archaeological Unit. Between 1987-89, during the process of undergrowth clearance and consolidation of the north wall, the original size and shape of the wall and the method of its construction were discovered. The results were subsequently published in the local archaeological journal Norfolk Archaeology (Davies 1991). In 1993, to the south of the site, a small car park was constructed and further investigation was carried out, involving a watching brief, and some metal-detector sampling.

In 1993 two larger-scale extra-mural surveys were set up. Fieldwalking was undertaken by a local amateur society, the Norfolk Archaeological and Historical Research Group (NAHRG), and this was complemented by a metal-detecting survey. Both were supervised by Museums Service staff. This became a useful exercise enabling the comparison of results from conventional fieldwalking and metal-detector recovery across the same areas. The latter survey turned-up metalwork of importance, including a number of La Tène style brooches, confirming the importance of the site during the late Iron Age, prior to the construction of the Roman town.

Presentation of the site
In addition to limited opportunities for fieldwork, background research into the site for its interpretation was undertaken, involving Museum and Norfolk Landscape Archaeology staff. As a result, a public information leaflet was prepared, which shows a reconstruction of the town, together with a brief text about the site and includes a fold-out plan. The public have been offered two alternative walks, which are distinguished by different colours on the leaflet. One, marked in red, follows the Roman town walls, geared to the history of the town, and takes about an hour. The other, marked in green, is a riverside walk and is routed to show more of the natural wildlife. This takes one-and-a half hours. The research also resulted in the preparation two reconstruction paintings of the Roman town, both by Sue White of Norfolk Landscape Archaeology. The first shows the whole town around the year AD 300 and the second is a detail of the earlier forum/basilica complex, based on excavation records of Professor Atkinson and their interpretation by Professor Frere (Frere 1971). A series of information panels, placed at strategic points on the pathways around the town provide an important element in the interpretation of the site for the general public. These were again designed by Sue White.

A special Caistor display was designed and set up at Norwich Castle Museum in 1993. Although permanent, this display was established to coincide with the opening of the site to the public. The intention has been to provide a history of the site through the presentation of artefacts from excavations at the town. Displays in three Edmonds cases are complemented by information panels illustrating aspects of life at the site and its development through from the Late Iron Age and early Roman military periods. Other artefacts from Caistor already form the basis of archaeological displays within the main Archaeology Gallery. In this way it is intended that visitors to the museum are encouraged to visit the site and that those to the site also be stimulated to visit the museum.

Other associated initiatives have been followed. The Museum Education Department has produced a Teachers' Pack, which includes a slide set, and which has been distributed to schools across Norfolk. A special education day was also held for teachers in order to inform them of the new resource being made available to them and to explain its history.

The running of the site
Caistor Roman town was officially opened to the public on the 10th June 1993 by Sir John Johnson, Chairman of the Countryside Commission, following ten years of gradual preparation and planning.
There are now regular tours around the site, both for the public and for special interest groups. A guide book is also in active preparation, which will make use of Castle Museum archive photography and illustrations. This work, at Caistor, is continuing. The Trust won five national awards for the project between 1994-95.

Since April 1995 the Trust has passed the routine management of the property over to South Norfolk District Council. In practice, much still needs to be done and solved. For example, there are a number of issues currently being addressed. The basic question of an on-site leaflet dispenser is problematic. This has had to be removed because of continued vandalism, which is a particular problem in an isolated rural location.

Additional facilities are needed on site, including toilets and a visitor centre. Basic plans for these have been submitted and discussions over their provision at the least intrusive location are still on-going. Other issues include the provision of highway signs and disabled access. For the latter, an all-weather flat path across selected parts of the site for wheelchair users is being laid and tested. This grass reinforcement surface is called Geoblock and was originally designed for use by larger wheeled vehicles. It has been chosen in order that sensitive archaeological layers beneath the surface are not disturbed.

Consultation with the public has repeatedly indicated that they would like to see a programme of excavation initiated at the site. It is felt by many visitors that open groundplans of buildings are important to convey more of an understanding of the town, which currently lies invisible beneath the surface. Plans for a limited campaign of excavation, which could also solve some of the most pressing questions of site dating, are now being prepared by the Norfolk Archaeological Unit.

The Caistor St Edmund Joint Advisory Board meets every six months and discusses progress with regard to these issues. This organisation comprises representatives from South Norfolk Council, local church and parish councils, the Norfolk Archaeological Trust and Norfolk Museums Service, as well as other local interest groups.

All of this work is proceeding in a climate of sensitivity towards local residents, who do not want their peaceful rural existence disturbed. If too much is done too quickly, the local infrastructure could not cope with the progress. Access roads would have to be widened and car parking facilities increased. This would all require increased funding. A balance between the interests of all parties must be maintained.

Burgh Castle
Burgh Castle is one of the best preserved and photogenic of Roman forts in Britain (Fig 2). The Roman fort is in a beautiful location just inland from Great Yarmouth, overlooking the River Waveney and Halvergate Marshes. The west side has fallen away into the marshes but the walls are otherwise almost complete and still stand to their original full height. It has a remarkable history. The fort was constructed in the late third or early fourth century and it gradually took over the role of principal Saxon Shore Fort at this location, from Caister-on-Sea, overlooking the Great Estuary which once occupied the area now silted-up and covered by the town of Yarmouth and surrounding marshes (Gurney 1996).

Roman occupation ceased at the end of the fourth century but there was subsequent Saxon activity within and to the east of the walls. A Norman motte and bailey

Castle was constructed within the fort in the 11th century. The site was the centre of thriving activity in the 19th century, with a brick and cement works next to the fort, associated with a nearby windmill, which is exciting local industrial archaeologists. The site, as a protective enclosure, also has a fascinating background of use during the late historic periods. Most recently, the surrounding fields were used as airfields and by anti-aircraft batteries during the two World Wars.

In March 1995 the Trust embarked on an even more challenging project with the acquisition of this Saxon Shore fort. An area covering some 90 acres was acquired. Again, a package was assembled involving the assistance of numerous bodies. Grants came from English Heritage, the Countryside Commission, the Broads Authority and the District and Parish Councils.

Involvement of the Norfolk Archaeological Trust
There has been low-key access to Burgh Castle for the public for some years. Now, the Trust's aim is to achieve an integrated management scheme to improve public access to the Roman fort, to improve site interpretation and to protect the setting of the monument. This requires the conservation of the surrounding land, including the freshwater reed beds and river bank.

A management plan was produced following detailed consultation with over twenty interested organisations. The Trust has been offered a Countryside Stewardship Scheme. Initial preparation for a developed site presentation has begun. The land has now been ploughed and a new heavy duty grass mix is beginning to come through.

Archaeological involvement
Some initial archaeological investigation has again preceded these developments. In 1994, excavation around the church to the east of the fort revealed a complex sequence of third and fourth century features cut into the subsoil. This work, together with interpretation of aerial photographs, has shown that there is up to 40 hectares of late Roman occupation in the vicinity.

Archaeological surveys have again been undertaken. The Norfolk Archaeological and Historical Research Group, and also Museum staff, with a surveyor from the Norfolk Archaeological Unit, have fieldwalked the site. There have been controlled metal detecting surveys over many months.

In advance of the site acquisition, conditions imposed on the purchasers stipulated that two metal detector rallies be held. Fortunately, these were managed impeccably, thanks to the cooperation of some detectorists who regularly work closely with Norwich Museum and who agreed to take on their organisation. Finds from the rallies were recorded and include mainly Roman, with some Saxon, artefacts and some 2000 Roman coins. All of this material is currently being integrated and prepared for a full archaeological study of the site.

Site interpretation
Site interpretation is currently being worked on, with

access. The RSPB and Norfolk Flora Society are also acting as advisors to the project. Once the site is properly functioning, the Parish Council will employ a temporary warden, in order to help safeguard the site.

Burgh Castle is situated just two miles west of Great Yarmouth. Yarmouth Museums, who are part of Norfolk Museums Service, will eventually create a display about the site, within an overall interpretation of the development of the Estuary and formation of Yar-

Fig 2 Burgh Castle, Norfolk. Aerial view of the Roman fort from the east. Photo: Derek A Edwards, Norfolk Air Photographs Library,Norfolk Museums Service)

equal emphasis given to the setting, ecology and wildlife, alongside the archaeology. This is a wetland area of international importance. With this in mind, staff in the Natural History Department of Norwich Castle Museum are helping the Field Archaeology Division with interpretation panel texts.

At present, there is a single English Heritage interpretation panel on site. Work on new interpretation panels has taken place, involving the Broads Authority and the Norfolk Archaeological Trust. Low-level, unobtrusive, panels are being designed which look like Roman masonry, when viewed from a distance. A new development in these panels will be a tactile element, for visually impaired and blind visitors. They will have a raised plan of the fort, so that people can trace the outline of walls, bastions and the landscape.

The Broads Authority is currently designing a car park and the District Council is providing advice on disabled

mouth. Archaeology Department staff will again be involved in a consultative capacity.

Tasburgh
In 1994 the Norfolk Archaeological Trust has also acquired a third archaeological site, at Tasburgh, to the south of Norwich. Some evidence for Iron Age and Saxon activity, in association with an earthwork, still leaves much interpretative work to be done on the nature of the site.

Conclusion
The involvement of museums with open-air sites presents a new dimension to the presentation and interpretation of local archaeology. The reasons underlying Norfolk's involvement in this work were essentially the result of initiatives to protect and conserve sites through their purchase by custodians. The results have seen an

enhanced public awareness and enjoyment of important local sites and a development of the role of Norfolk Museums Service staff beyond the confines of traditional museum interpretation work.

With regard to the protection of the sites, acquisition can be seen to be one of the most effective and beneficial methods. The alternative of scheduling monuments has limitations (Wade-Martins 1996). It does not protect the immediate setting; neither does it provide an interpretation for visitors. Most scheduled monuments are also in private ownership, allowing only limited public access.

The work described above was achieved through the agency of many organisations. Staff of the Norfolk Museums Service have been involved in various roles within these initiatives and have supported the Norfolk Archaeological Trust in this most valuable work.

References

Davies, J A 1991 Excavations at the north wall, Caistor St Edmund, 1987-89 *Norfolk Archaeology* XLI iii, 325-337

Frere, S S 1971 The forum and baths at Caistor by Norwich *Britannia* II, 1-26

Gurney, D 1996 The 'Saxon Shore' in Norfolk, in Margeson, S, Ayers, B and Heywood, S (eds) *A Festival of Norfolk Archaeology* Hunstanton, 30-39

Wade-Martins, P July 1996 Monument conservation through land purchase *Conservation Bulletin* 8-11

THE DEFENCE OF BRITAIN PROJECT: PROGRESS TO DATE

Jim Earle, The Defence of Britain Project

A philosophical luminary once remarked that the tree in his Oxford quadrangle remained a tree even when nobody was conscious of it. The same observation might usefully be made about The Defence of Britain project when enquirers ask, with gratifying frequency, about its latest discoveries.

The answer, of course, is that the project has only "discovered" military archaeology in the sense that Columbus "discovered" America. Militiary concrete, like America, has been around for some considerable time and its allegedly recent discovery has really been a process of widening awareness beyond a handful of indians. In the course of charting this archaeological New World, the project has been guided by fiercely independent and knowledgeable tribes of amateurs who roamed the concrete plains of Britain's recent defence heritage long before the arrival of the first professional archaeologist.

The analogy may be extended because we endured, at an early stage, our own version of the Indian Wars. Contact between professional and amateur remains cautious but, generally speaking, good relations with the natives are obviously beneficial to both sides. Had this not been the case, the project would undoubtedly have perished in its first winter, long before the topsails of financial salvation - in the form of a Lottery galleon - pierced the horizon.

Whilst the project cannot claim discoveries, it has brought a few curiosities - the mermaids and narwhals' teeth of military archaeology - before an interested public. First amongst these were coastal sound mirrors, enormous acoustic devices from pre-radar days when many people believed that "the bomber will always get through". Although they were obsolescent by 1935, these surreal structures still guard parts of the Kentish and Cumbrian coasts. We persuaded the Sunday Telegraph Magazine to carry an article about the mirrors last year and they recently featured in a television advertisement of such astonishing subtlety that no-one could identify the product.

The extent to which The Defence of Britain project can claim credit for the interest that now surrounds these acoustic relics is a moot point; the fact remains that their importance is widely acknowledged and they are no longer obscure curiosities prone to thoughtless demolition.

Even less well-known, until recently, were the hides and communications installations of a putative British Resistance Organisation. Created durinig the darkest days of World War II, the so-called Auxiliary Units were trained to fight a guerrilla war in the aftermath of German invasion. For obvious reasons, their existence was cloaked in secrecy which remains habitual for many veterans even today. The hides - elaborately concealed and often equipped with sophisticated ventilation systems - are being re-discovered, while the would-be guerrillas are increasingly prepared to record their stories on film for The Defence of Britain project. The occupants of "Churchill's last ditch" were under no illusions about the reliability of their compatriots under interrogation. In the event of invasion, many units would have included local gamekeepers and others who "knew too much" amongst their earliest victims.

Much larger underground structures, such as the enormous Second World War factory at Drayclot near Kidderminster, are also being investigated and recorded on film. The Drayclot factory produced a number of light engineering products including components for the Pegasus aero-engine which powered Sunderland flying boats. A white narcotic-like by-product, cyanide, was assiduously collected by some of the workers and sold to black American troops in Kidderminster for three shillings a bag. Such reminiscences, inseparable from the task of recording redundant military sites, allow few cosy illusions about the "Special Relationship" at its less elevated levels.

The selfless determination that drove so much of Britain's military endeavour has proved an unfailing cure for cynicism. Near Watford in Hertfordshire, behind the Buildings Research Establishment, a 1:50 scale model of the Möhne Dam survives from extensive tests which preceded the famous "Dambusters Raid". The model consists of 600,000 scale mortar cubes set by hand in lime-based cement during the winter of 1940. The builders completed their work, often crouched in icy water all night with fingers flayed by the lime, in just seven weeks. When the dam was breached during tests, allotment holders down-stream were mystified by the sudden flood which destroyed their crops.

The defensive effort was financial as well as physical. By September 1941, Eastern Command had spent £3,745,000 on 5,819 pillboxes while Southern Command had built or planned 3,242 similar structures for £3,845,000. At the end of the war, Worthing alone had five pillboxes and 66 anti-tank blocks on every mile of its sea-front. When the time came to demolish them, each pillbox required the attentions of a foreman, three hammermen and three labourers for almost a fortnight. The Defence of Britain project, bolstered by the archival research of Dr Colin Dobinson, is now well-advanced in the task of recording those anti-invasion defences which survive.

Fig 1 Pillbox on the coast at Kilnsea, Cumbria
Photo: Roger Thomas RCHME

There is a theory that individuals and societies need an opponent against which to define themselves. With the menace of German aggression removed, the great powers poured immense energy into a Cold War whose legacy of built structures must yet be fully revealed. According to one Defence of Britain project correspondent, a former secretary to the United Kingdom Chiefs of Staff, great efforts were made to save money by refurbishing the underground structures of one war for use in the next. Unfortunately for the tax-payer, the great majority of pre-1945 "holes in the ground" were either unsafe or contaminated by asbestos. Others, including the reserve GHQ Land under Wentworth Golf Course, had been so comprehensively stripped out that refurbishment was uneconomic. The Cold Warriors observed, in the course of their search for new underground premises, that southern England was already perforated to a point where they felt unsafe on the surface.

Increasing numbers of Cold War structures, in particular the cavernous Regional Seats of Government and former Rotor radar bunkers, are now falling into private hands. Many of these are serving as document stores or museums, but in some cases a peaceful usage is hard to discern. At Orfordness, the National Trust presides over a "philosophy of dereliction" which - in the course of several centuries - may lay to rest a significant legacy of Britain's ultimate deterrent. For now, massive concrete pagodas - which once housed all manner of tests for the components of nuclear weapons - brood menacingly across the Suffolk coast. There is no shortage of time in which to record these leviathans. Meanwhile, it is reassuring to know that Armageddon was never meant to arrive by accident.

Inevitably, there are some types of defensive site which prove more interesting than others and which become personal favourites. At the turn of the century, the chronological starting point for The Defence of Britain project, fear of invasion led to the construction of mobilisation depots around London so that militias could guard the capital more effectively. One of the earliest and largest examples survives, despite the assiduous work of vandals, at North Weald in Essex. There can be few better documented examples of xenophobic reaction to national decline; all of the original draughtsman's plans are lodged in the Public Record Office and the redoubt features in William Le Queux's fictional account, "The Invasion of 1910". The site is a scheduled monument and we hope that a Management Proposal, drafted by Defence of Britain project staff, will eventually lead to its restoration and the installation of a public exhibition on the military defence of London.

Many of these sites have already been the subject of extensive research and some were moderately well-known long before The Defence of Britain project began its survey. The project's great strength is an ability to extend awareness of Britain's defence heritage whilst involving people from all walks of life in the task of recording it. In the process, we are already identifying questions which ought to inspire and guide more detailed future research.

Fig 2 Royal Naval Hospital, Haslar, Hampshire
Photo: RCHME

Fifty years ago the concept of "industrial archaeology" was equally new and regarded with much the same scepticism that surrounded The Defence of Britain project in its early days. If the project can help to establish a new archaeological discipline, founded upon a broad base of genuine public interest and participation, then it may be a truly worthy memorial to the industrialised carnage of a turbulent century.

Note
Additional information is available from the Project Office at the Imperial War Museum, Duxford Airfield, Cambridge CB2 4QR. Tel: 01223 830280

IT IN MUSEUM DISPLAYS - THE NEXT *N* YEARS

Edmund Southworth, Liverpool Museum, National Museums and Galleries on Merseyside

I was grateful for the invitation to address the SMA conference on the topic of the future development of IT in museum displays but also amused by the opportunity to speculate on the future. I am reasonably well qualified to speak on the use of IT in museums. It has been an essential part of my professional life as a museum curator since the early 1980s and the National Museums and Galleries has a pretty good track record in the innovative use of new technologies. What I never told the organisers of the conference, though, was that since I was about ten years old I had been an avid reader of science fiction in all shapes and sizes. I actively collect early paperback pulp science fiction and have been known to watch the odd Star Trek movie or two. I state that, not as some kind of cathartic confession of a sad existence, but to say that I know more than many people the difficulties of predicting the future. Ever since the early 1800s writers have used their imagination to extrapolate from the known technology of their period to the near or far future. The 1940s and 50s were a time when science fiction authors successfully predicted space travel, robots, computers, organ transplants, genetic modifications etc. They also predicted invasions from Mars, safe nuclear power, time travel, interstellar travel, the end to poverty and disease. On the whole they failed to predict the end of apartheid and the pot noodle.

The conference theme was landscape and this paper tries to set IT in that context. It is an attempt to extrapolate from the known to the unknown, via the fairly predictable. One thing I can safely predict is that the pace of change in information technology will continue to accelerate; that this paper will be out of date before it is published, and that you will probably have already seen adverts in the press for products which I was only speculating about at the conference.

Landscape archaeology and museums
The more I think about it the less convinced I am that the museum display is the best way of understanding archaeology. We all live in a place. We tend to work in another place. We travel from one place to another during our daily lives. Our perception of our quality of life is bound up in our surroundings, whether they be urban or rural. Archaeology is one of the most valuable tools for understanding the landscape around us. As we discover more and more sites, particularly through the use of aerial photography and geo-physical techniques, we can build up a better picture of the changes in our landscape. A landscape is tangible, and it is easier for us to relate to our ancestors if we can imagine them in our landscape and see how they have modified it for us. In the same way that a stone axe has more relevance if we can imagine the hunter using it, we can see the impact that farmers, builders, engineers have had on the land. But in order to do this you have to feel part of that landscape.

I recently visited a number of visitor centres in Denmark and Ireland as part of an EU research programme. Nowhere was the tension between place and buildings greater than in the Aran Islands of the West coast of Ireland. The great iron age fort of Dun Aenghus, on a cliff-top site, with hardly a label in sight, was crowded with visitors. Standing within a few inches of a 300 foot drop without any safety railings is a powerful emotional experience. The brand new heritage and interpretation centre for the island, built a mile or so away in a council depot with EU funding, was very competent but empty and soul-less by comparison. The challenge for new technology is to bridge that gap. Will it rise to the challenge?

Survey of present
What is the current state of play with gallery-based displays? For the most part we have updated our presentation tools. I suspect the conventional 35mm slide show is dead(ish). Long live the video! Video tape presentations are now fairly common. The quality of videos varies dramatically and it is does not entirely correlate with the amount of money spent. Video is best with moving images and simply converting a slide show of still images is not using the technology to best advantage. Rather than tape players many museums are moving to video disc players which are more expensive to start with but cheaper to run.

Interestingly the "Peppers Ghost" seems to be making a come-back as a visual aid; presumably because it is cheap, reliable and effective.

Museums have never been very good with sound and the sound of a landscape is a bit subtle. The human voice though is a very powerful communicator and is surely preferable to written text. Until recently the only way of delivering sound has been through audio tape players of varying descriptions. They were unreliable and quality depended on how much you spent! The digital revolution which brought us audio CD-ROMs and talking lifts has made sound much more accessible and far cheaper. The audio tape is fast dying out and sound wands and their static equivalent are widely used and marketed. The potential of integrating the human voice (in several languages) with music and sound effects should not be lost on curators and designers.

As an aside, in saying this I am aware that many of these technologies are only in use in newer galleries, larger institutions or richer ones. In the context of this paper I was asked to look at what is possible; not what is in general use.

Multimedia

There have been a number of surveys of multimedia in museums over the last few years and exhibits which feature multimedia have a disturbing air of fashion about them. They do vary in quality tremendously. At the risk of attempting a definition, multimedia is the integration of data, words, pictures and sound with varying levels of interaction with the visitor. As the tools for producing multimedia presentations have improved, so it has become easier for such presentations to be done in house. What is actually happening is that companies are springing up everywhere offering their services. I'm actually old-fashioned enough to say that you tend to get a better product by splitting content from presentation. If you take the example of a book. Authors do what they are best at; writing. The publisher and printer convert that script into a book using their own, usually considerable, expertise. If author and publisher respect each others professional expertise then you get a creative partnership which works well. In recent years Desk Top Publishing has allowed authors to produce their own work. In general terms (and there are many honourable exceptions) the end products are not as good though they are usually cheaper because the author's time is either discounted or subsidised.

In the same way multimedia works best as a creative partnership where each party knows what is expected of the other and understands what the other does. The real danger with multimedia is that style overcomes content. This is heightened by that fact that many multimedia companies employ young geniuses who will happily work through the night to create what they consider to be a masterpiece. The content rapidly takes a back seat in these circumstances.

Archaeological tools

It is important in this discussion about museum display to be aware of how IT is impacting on the rest of the profession. If we see the display in the museum as just one component of an integrated archaeological continuum that includes development control, SMRs, fieldwork, post-excavation and publication etc, then we need to look at the data which is being produced all through these various processes. How is it produced, on what equipment and for what purpose? Can we re-use that data for our purposes? I would quote (if it wasn't too embarrassing) a Scottish excavation unit which has one of the country's best integrated systems for dealing with excavation archives. The local museum where the archive is deposited has no such system and years of work by the unit is virtually unusable by the museum. What a waste.

As one example only, the use of Autocad for site planning is now widespread in excavation units. How many museum displays integrate three-dimensional computerised reconstruction based on that excavation data? I suspect few. Other techniques such as GIS and digital terrain modelling are becoming more widespread and we should be looking at how we exploit the data that other people are developing.

Developing technologies

Video. In my view the technology which offers significant potential in the very near future is video. Digital video is capable of manipulation and computer control. Already we have video projectors and larger and flatter screens are appearing all the time. Video can be edited on PC-based systems and integrated with other types of data. If a picture is worth a thousand words, then a moving image with high quality sound is worth far more. Television has not killed cinema but I think digital video will seriously injure the traditional museum label!

Internet. This is the subject that has occupied more column inches in the press in the last year than any other and I don't propose to discuss it here in detail. Suffice it to say that it is here to stay and it will become more and more pervasive. It would be facile to say that the sum of all human knowledge is there but it sometimes seems that way when you are looking for something specific! At Liverpool Museum I have run a few sessions for the public where I guide visitors through selected WWW "sites". *Romans on the Information Superhighway* was particularly popular. I was able to show people animated 3-D models of buildings in Pompeii, photographs of Hadrian's Wall, a guided tour of Caistor-by-Norwich etc. Bill Gates (and the fact I don't have to explain who he is in an archaeological publication is significant) sees the Internet as the biggest marketplace ever invented. In this aspect - as in so much of IT - museums have no impact on the market and we will follow developments meekly rather than innovate.

Most museums discuss the Internet at the moment in terms of providing their own information on the World Wide Web and there is gentle competition as to who can get the best sites up and running. Whilst this is important I feel museums have a more significant role in bringing together intelligible strands from this world-wide mass of information and acting as a channel of communication between data and its users.

Virtual reality

One could say there is no such thing as reality. It all depends on how you look at things. We each experience reality in different ways and some of us can suspend disbelief better than others. Most of the exhibits called virtual reality are poor quality three dimensional models which one can view either on a headset - so-called immersive reality - or on a flat screen of some kind. Some things model better than others. Buildings model well. Landscapes model well at a larger scale. The so-called fly-by, which recreates the view from a helicopter, aeroplane (or alien spaceship!) works very well. The proper description for this approach is simulation. It resembles the real thing but an altogether more honest approach would be to declare the assumptions and failings underlying the simulation. Most reconstruction of buildings, for example, fail to discuss the wide variety of options for roofing that are equally possible from the same set of foundations.

Smart Cards. The technology for recording small chunks of information on paper or plastic cards cheaply is well understood and used in phone cards, credit cards and railway tickets. A typical use is the supermarket loyalty card which enables the shop to build up a picture of which goods every shopper takes home. A number of museums have used the technology to give each visitor the ability to interact on an individual basis with

exhibits. One can imagine "personalising" a visit by extracting information about the exact place the visitor lives.

NMGM initiatives

The National Museums and Galleries on Merseyside is at the forefront of integrating these various techniques. The JASON project, mentioned in a previous paper, was the first to use satellite technology to broadcast live scientific expeditions from places such as Hawaii into museums and science centres across the US. NMGM is the European node in the network. The project now incorporates satellite, Internet and phone communications to allow museum visitors in Liverpool to put questions to workers out in the field. There have been few archaeological applications - the project has concentrated on spectacular phenomenon such as volcanoes and coral reefs - but it has allowed us to develop our use of the technology.

Locally we are developing a project called *Sands of Time* with three local authorities and the English Tourist Board. The subject of a Millennium bid, it may develop in various ways, but the principle of the scheme involves establishing remote TV cameras at sensitive coastal wildlife sites and linking them all together with high speed telecommunications, using the museum as a focal point. We will integrate other information, such as the Merseyside Sites and Monuments Record and other environmental data, and transmit programmes to schools via, for example, the local cable TV network or the Internet.

NMGM has recently installed video-conferencing equipment funded by BT as part of the MuseNet initiative to encourage museums to use this technology and talk to each other more. Within the museums we have installed video-links to connect front of house with behind the scenes. The newly-opened (October 1996) Conservation Centre has cabling connecting an auditorium to conservation laboratories. At set times a conservator appears live before an audience and explains what they are working on. The camera is operator controlled and can focus in on the specimens on the bench. The "performance" is hosted by a demonstrator who encourages the audience to participate in the dialogue. This concept was developed in Liverpool Museum and is being well received.

One of the galleries to feature in the new Liverpool Museum development plan (and inevitable lottery bid) will be on the subject of the archaeology and landscape of the Mersey region over the last 10,000 years. Still some years away from construction, the gallery will benefit from all these experiments in telecommunications which bring landscape into the building and allow the museum visitor to "visit" another place, whether this is the outside world or a workspace elsewhere in the building.

The Future

It is beyond the scope of this paper to predict how every aspect of IT or museum display techniques might change in the future. I can give some suggestions though. In terms of hardware it seems to be established that the processing power of computer chips doubles in 18 months. The price remains the same or less in real terms. Higher processing speeds, larger memories, faster transfer of data from storage media, higher resolution displays. All these are predictable in that we know these are developed in the research laboratories and will be on the market soon. We should realise that the hardware is not just in computers. Digital cameras, digital phones, digital television etc all use related technologies. One of the important concepts is convergence. It is a mistake to see video as somehow different from computing, to see the telephone as different from a computer network. Digital information can be captured, manipulated, stored or communicated in similar and related ways. Whether the inputs and outputs are speech, music, film, photographs, graphs, books etc is immaterial. This tendency will increase.

In a market economy the industry will be dominated by the more successful companies and the products they support. Quality is not necessarily the defining criterion. There will be fewer and fewer packages in everyday use. This creates problems if you want something different; but a bonus is standardisation by default. I was at meeting recently with a representative of RCHME who was describing a pilot study for a major data collection exercise. The pilot was done in dBase IV but the main project would probably use Microsoft Access. Five years ago, or less, it would have been assumed that purpose built software would have to be written. Ten years ago the rest of any such meeting would have been dominated by a discussion about standards. One might think the corollary of this would be that there is no room for individual initiative and that everything will look the same in the future. In practice programming has become far easier, with languages like Visual Basic. Some of the multimedia authoring tools currently on the market allow the most sophisticated video effects that wouldn't disgrace the BBC of a few years ago.

Another by-product of this domination by a few packages will be that communication between software applications and different machines will become increasingly easier. One of the dreams of early museums documentation was that computers could talk to each other and that information could be gathered together from different machines in different parts of the country. What we forget when talking about the Internet is that there are hundreds and thousands of private networks already in existence. Most larger institutions network their computers together to share information and equipment. This can be within a building or between buildings. Our internal phone system in Liverpool uses a microwave link across the city to the Maritime Museum. It has enough capacity to take data as well. Bank cashpoint machines talk to head office, national lottery machines talk to Camelot, and so on. The Universities SuperJanet network is already capable of transmitting live high quality video across the country so that a surgeon in one part of the country can supervise an operation in another. This technology is available now. The use we are most familiar with is video-conferencing but the same technology can broadcast an excavation live into the museum gallery. The excavation doesn't have to be in this country.

So what will a museum display look like in *n* years time where *n* is any number between one and ten. The answer is that in broad outline most displays will probably look much the same as they do now. I would hope that people introduce the new technologies with some sensitivity and thought. I have seen a number of displays, not all archaeological, which are powerful arguments for not using new technology at all. There is a director of a national museum who has, allegedly, forbidden computer screens in his galleries. I think that is an extreme view but I can understand scepticism about their benefits. We have to keep in mind what the public wants and has at home. Most of them already have TVs and Videos and a short attention span. They don't read encyclopaedias for enjoyment at home; they are unlikely to want to read multimedia encyclopaedias at the museum, especially if they have to stand up to do it! At the same time increasing numbers of people will have Internet access at home or school. Some types of information should be available to them without visiting the museum.

In our galleries...

- We will gain a window on the landscape as it is now by using large scale video. This will act as wallpaper. This is one of the techniques that works well at *Evolution of Wales* geology display at Cardiff.

- We will be recreating our interpretation of past landscapes on screens or walls. This will combine 3D contour mapping and CAD images to recreate real sites in real landscapes as they might have been. We will populate these landscapes with computer-generated "people" who will interact with the virtual world they live in.

- We will give visitors access to SMRs and the like in graphical and interactive form. You will see what your street was like 100 or 1000 years ago. You will talk to this SMR and it will answer you.

- You will interact with the labels. One of your party will carry around a magic wand. This will tell you where you are in the museum and remind you if you have missed something important. It will pick up text, sound and pictures as you pass by the display case. It will remind you how these objects relate to those you walked past earlier, or the last time you visited.

- At a point in the gallery you will see what has been discovered today in the excavation on the other side of the county. A live video-link will show you the pot sherds being washed by a rather scruffy individual with a ring through his nose. At 3pm the Director of the excavation will give a guided tour of the site. It will be chucking it down with rain but because of the live video link you don't need to get your wheelchair stuck in the mud.

- The research area at the end of the gallery will be open for you to consult the archives. Not only can you check what is in the museum collections, but you can retrieve the 1950s aerial photographs of the site that you have just "visited". You can talk by video-phone to the finds researcher in Australia who has been working on the post-medieval ceramics from the site.

- On the way out you swipe your ecash card through the donations box terminal and the robotic figure of Tim Schadla-Hall says thank you and tells you to come back again soon.

I hinted in the abstract at a set of rules or guidelines for the use of IT in museum displays. All I would say is that in this rapidly changing field inflexible rules are a bad thing and you should encourage creativity in interpreting the rules or ignoring them altogether.

- Always overestimate the time and budget needed for doing IT projects. It is an industry known statistic that only 16% of IT projects are ever completed on time. Even fewer are completed on budget. This is unlikely to change.

- Always overestimate the maintenance costs budget for IT projects.

- Build prototypes and evaluate how effective they are. Remember that IT equipment goes out of date within a few months but it is usually so reliable that it is with you for years. And you won't be able to replace it. Get it right first time.

- Keep experimenting. Lock the youngest member of your IT staff in the basement with the latest software and see what they come up with.

- Don't throw the museum objects away - you will need them for when people get tired of virtual reality and want real reality.

Conclusion

Our challenge is to get people inside a building, give them an understanding of landscape and motivate them sufficiently to go out for themselves and experience it. We need to equip them with some rudimentary skills so they can analyse and understand what they are looking at. What we do should be complementary and not a substitute. We should not attempt to re-create landscape within buildings.

There can be little doubt that information and communications technology has the potential to interpret landscape in new ways. I feel that we are on the brink of a period of substantial change in the relationship of museum displays to the outside world. We do not fully understand the potential of these new tools. Some of the things we build with them will not work well. Some of our tools will become obsolete quickly; others will develop and become everyday and familiar. Those that have the tools will progress much faster than those who do not. This same group of people will make mistakes and some of these will be expensive. There will be those who yearn for the bygone age of objects in cases. They will have powerful arguments on their side.

I said at the beginning that predicting the future is difficult. One thing is certain - that nothing is certain!

SPECTRUM: A RAY OF LIGHT FOR ARCHAEOLOGISTS

Christine Longworth, Liverpool Museum, National Museums and Galleries on Merseyside

SPECTRUM: The UK Museum Documentation Standard was published by the MDA in 1994. It is a resource that brings together the wide range of activities which are carried out by museums, from dealing with public enquiries to holding major exhibitions, and provides a comprehensive checklist for carrying out that work. Every museum, whatever its size or type, needs to know what it has, where it can be found, who owns it, and a host of other requirements. 1994 SPECTRUM defines the minimum standards for collections management documentation for all museum disciplines, including Archaeology. The SPECTRUM documentation system can be applied to a computer database or a paper-based system, whichever is appropriate for individual museums. It is intended as a recommended standard documentation system that museums can use to select the most appropriate sections for their own use.

1994 SPECTRUM is divided into the following 20 separate procedures:

- Object entry
- Loans in
- Acquisition
- Inventory control
- Location & movement control
- Cataloguing
- Condition checking
- Conservation
- Reproduction
- Risk management
- Insurance management
- Indemnity management
- Valuation control
- Audit
- Exhibitions & displays
- Despatch
- Loans out
- Loss
- Deaccession & disposal
- Retrospective documentation

Each procedure is laid out in the same way:

Definition: explains the scope of the procedure and any ambiguous terms.
Minimum Standard: what each institution should achieve.
Procedure: the recommended way of achieving the minimum standard.
Notes: where detailed explanation is required, the information is provided here, including advice on legal and policy issues.
Sources of advice and help: bibliographic references and organisations providing information about the procedure.
Relevant units of information: used to support the procedures, together with a description of how they fit together to create a record.

At the beginning of 1996 a number of subject-specific working parties were set up by the MDA to refine SPECTRUM and provide a detailed guide on particular museum requirements, including Archaeology, Collections Management, Conservation and Social History. The brief for Archaeology was to present an archaeological slant and identify minimum standards for all types of archaeological collections. The target user-groups would be all those concerned with the care and use of archaeological collections in museums and other organisations which adopt museum standards, whether in a general or specialist capacity. "Other organisations" covers archaeological field units and research projects which are instumental in the creation of archaeological archives, and university and related teaching collections if not already in a museum. Suppliers of software and data systems managers were also considered to be potential users.

To ensure that the views of the archaeological community were reflected in the archaeology guide to SPECTRUM, contact with relevant organisations was made in three ways:

- direct representation on the working party
- coordination with other MDA SPECTRUM working parties
- contact with other specialist archaeological groups.

Cross-references and bibliographic details of other relevant guidelines and standards are incorporated within particular sections.

The existing 20 procedures were devised for general museum use. It was clear that major changes and additions were required for the new guide. The principal reason for this was because archaeological archives, particularly those generated by fieldwork, produce a very different assortment of material from the traditional museum collection.

There are two distinct elements to the archives, the finds and the documentary archive. The finds archive includes individual objects, bulk assemblages and environmental remains. The documentary archive contains all the drawn and written evidence from the site and the research archive. Photographs and digital data are also part of the documentary archive.

The most consistent omission from all the existing procedures was the mention of documentary archive. In the context of archaeological collections, the documentary archive is as important as the finds and should be fully recorded and curated.

Copyright and Transfer of Title are very important issues where archaeological excavation archives are concerned and have been highlighted in the Archaeology guide. They are very complex but by following the procedures outlined in the guide and by referring to the bibliography, it should be possible to cover most situations.

The receiving institution must obtain copyright in the documentary archive either by assignment, or if this is not possible, by licence (SMA 1995). In England and Wales, the agreement of the owner of the finds should be sought at the earliest opportunity. In Scotland, the finds archive is owned by the Crown and different arrangements exist for transfer. Separate Transfer of Title documents are required for the finds archive and the documentary archive. With the exception of archaeological projects in Scotland, the owner of the finds archive is usually the landowner. The person who created the documentary archive is the owner of the copyright. The main exception is where a person creates a copyright work in the course of his/her employment, and the employer retains the copyright.

If a museum does not own copyright, or have a licence, it cannot provide public access to that material. This means that it cannot be copied, including loading onto a computer; copies cannot be issued to the public; it cannot be used in a display and it cannot be sent out on loan. It can be used for study and research (Wienand 1996).

The MGC laid down clear guidelines in its 1992 publication "The museum should assign a global identity number to the whole site, ideally before excavation starts......Any *bone fide* enquirer must ... be allowed to inspect objects and archives from the collections".

The SMA in its 1995 guidelines, reiterated the above and added "Long-term public access to the archive should be guaranteed, and the archives use should be actively encouraged".

To quote from The Museums Association Code of Practice "The governing body should ensure that its museum services are physically and intellectually accessible to the public on a regular basis. It should also ensure that members of the public have reasonable access to members of staff, to information about the collections and to the collections, whether displayed or not".

To comply with these requirements, there are procedures which must be carried out before an archive is deposited in a museum and, once in the museum, public access must be guaranteed. To ensure that museums carry out these procedures, the working party has recommended the inclusion of two new procedures, Pre-Entry and Collections Access and Use, along with amendments to the existing procedures.

The Pre-Entry requirement is to provide the museum with essential information for planning the acquisition and curation of the archive. The museum curator should liaise with excavators at an early stage to ensure that the excavating body understands the museums collecting policy and the museums conditions for deposition of archaeological archives. An expected date of deposition should be agreed, a museum accession number (or equivalent) allocated and the museum should be informed of the anticipated quantity and type of material from the excavation.

It is only recently, especially since guidelines such as the *Standards in the Museum Care of Archaeological Collections (MGC 1992)* and *Towards an Accessible Archaeological Archive: The Transfer of Archaeological Archives to Museums* (SMA 1995) highlighted the need, that individual museums have started to issue their own guidelines for the deposition of excavation archives. In the past, museums received archives with little or no control over the quantity or quality of the archive. Finds may have been boxed in a variety of containers, badly labelled or not labelled at all. The documentary archive ranged from detailed analysis of every sherd to no documentary archive at all. The result of this was that archives were inaccessible to everyone, including the curators charged with the responsibility of looking after them. By standardising the requirements and issuing guidelines to excavators at the beginning of all fieldwork, the problems of the past can be avoided and the archives will become accessible.

There is still a big gap between field archaeologists and museum archaeologists. Planning archaeologists have a role in alerting the excavators to the new guidelines for the transfer of excavation archives. There is a need to train and educate the field archaeologists into why museums need the archives in an accessible format.

Collections Access is a procedure to document and manage any uses of the objects and documentary archive by museum staff or the public. This is the procedure that fulfils the access requirement of the MGC. By following the procedures, access to confidential or sensitive information, eg location or value of objects, can be controlled while providing a complete record of the use made of the collections and of the enquirer.

This paper is not the place to detail all the new information. Some of the more important issues have been highlighted here. One important topic still under discussion is whether or not to separate out current and backlog archives. It is believed that some of the more complex procedures would become more manageable by separating them in this way. Case studies are included when necessary to explain more complex issues. It is anticipated that the subject-related guides to SPECTRUM will be published later this year.

References
Museums and Galleries Commission 1992 *Standards in the Museum Care of Archaeological Collections* MGC

Society of Museum Archaeologists 1995 *Towards an Accessible Archaeological Archive. The Transfer of Archaeological Archives to Museums: Guidelines for Use in England, Northern Ireland, Scotland and Wales First Edition* SMA

Wienand, Peter 1996 Transferring Intellectual Property Rights in the Archaeological Archive, in *Archaeology, Museums and the Law* Department of Museum Studies, University of Leicester

COPYRIGHT AND ACCESS

Neil Beagrie, Arts and Humanities Data Service, King's College, London

Copyright is central to any policy of access to museum collections. Any museum wishing to expand public access or to generate revenue to supplement it's core public funding must consider copyright as a pre-requisite for achieving these aims. An understanding of copyright is therefore increasingly essential for every professional museum archaeologist.

This paper outlines the major areas that museum archaeologists should consider in addressing copyright. It focuses on significant issues and current or impending changes to copyright law and their potential impact on museum activities. Copyright law and its application is complex and in many cases there will be exceptions and qualifications to the outline statements given here. More detailed sources of advice and guidance are therefore given at the end of the paper. Please note that specific legal advice must always be taken by individuals and institutions and this paper does not constitute legal advice by the author, or his employer.

What is copyright ?

Copyright is an intellectual property right, which can be sold, transferred or licensed. It exists automatically and there is no need for registration. It can therefore be difficult or impossible to find out who is the current copyright owner of a particular item. It is also possible for several different forms of copyright to exist in a single object, eg a book can have separate copyrights in the text and photographs as well as the copyright in the arrangement held by the publisher.

Copyright exists in original works and copies will only have a secondary copyright if skill and judgment is used in their creation. This is important in museums in two areas. Within museums photographing an out of copyright object can create a new copyright. This copyrighted image can then be used for reproduction and additional revenue. Secondly in an electronic context a separate copyright from the original can exist in a digital image if skill and judgment are involved in its creation. Awareness of this potential additional copyright in any digital image is important in granting permission or awarding contracts for imaging projects to ensure this copyright is not inadvertently given away to others.

Ownership of Copyright

Ownership of copyright is usually vested in the author of a work. There are two principal exceptions:

- Where an employee in the course of their employment creates a "work", their employer holds copyright

- Where an agreement exists transferring copyright from the author to someone else

Authorship is defined by the type of copyright and can be the person who creates the work or makes the necessary arrangements (eg a publisher).

It is also important to recognise that if work is not undertaken by a museum employee but by a contractor then the contractor has the copyright unless the contract specifically assigns the copyright to the museum.

Similarly curators should note that physical ownership of an item is separate from any copyright associated with it. Hence possession and ownership of a physical item, eg an archive or painting, does not itself mean a museum has the copyright and rights to use it. Care is therefore needed in accessioning new material to obtain both legal title and copyright. The SMA itself has published excellent guidance addressing this issue (Owen 1995, 14-19 and 61-67).

It is important for individual archaeologists to be aware of the rights of their employer in any work they create during their employment and equally for employers to be aware of the copyright implications of voluntary work or of unpaid and unofficial overtime by employees!

If legal ownership of any archaeological work is unclear or is excessively fragmented, it may be impossible for a museum to actively disseminate or use that work in the future. It is vital therefore for anyone involved in an archaeological project who has a potential copyright ownership or part ownership of datasets and other works created by that project to agree at the outset as to how the rights are to be held and any benefits shared.

Crown copyright

A unique feature of copyright in the UK compared to other countries is the existence of Crown copyright and Crown copyright is important for many archaeological archives as many of them are subject to it, having been produced or funded by government departments.

Under the 1988 Copyright, Designs and Patents Act (HMSO 1988) all works made by Her Majesty or by an officer or servant of the Crown in the course of his or her duties are governed by Crown copyright.

Prior to the 1988 Act the definition of Crown copyright was much wider. The 1911 Copyright Act gave copyright to the Crown in any work prepared or published by, or under the direction or control of the Crown, and also covered any "Crown" works created before the Act came into force. The 1956 Act replaced this with slightly more elaborate provisions. Essentially it established Crown copyright in: all works made by or under the direction or control of the Crown; and all works first published by or under the direction of the Crown (hence all works published by HMSO became Crown copyright even if the authors had no connection with the Crown in any other way).

Crown copyright is of considerable importance for archaeologists in the UK as most archaeological work prior to the 1980's was funded by the government, or is now undertaken by government bodies covered by Crown copyright such as RCHME. The provisions of Crown copyright therefore cover many archaeological archives and publications. It is worth noting however that the 1983 Act establishing English Heritage specifically states its employees are not to be considered as Crown servants and for this reason Crown copyright does not apply to any of EH's work produced since 1983. It remained in force however for all material produced by bodies it succeeded such as the DOE Inspectorate, MOW, etc. Similarly the major national museums covered by the 1983 Heritage Act also achieved independent copyright from that date.

All Crown copyrights are held by the Controller of HMSO and individual departments have delegated control for its administration(often closely proscribed) for materials held or produced by themselves. Crown copyright is not normally assigned to others but licensed. Different arrangements for Crown copyright administration exist for the Ordnance Survey and Hydrographic Office and these bodies in effect have sole responsibility for their Crown copyright materials.

An interesting anomaly has arisen because of the uniqueness of Crown copyright. EEC copyright directives could not accommodate it and therefore the duration of Crown copyright has been unaffected by the EEC Copyright Term Directive. Crown copyright therefore still remains valid for 50 years in published material and 125 years in unpublished material.

Moral rights

The 1988 Act introduced a series of "moral rights" usually exercisable by the author or his/her heirs. These are as follows:

- Paternity- the right to be identified as the author or director of a work

- Integrity- the right to object to the derogatory treatment of the author's work or its false attribution

- Privacy- the right to privacy in relation to photographs and films commissioned for private and domestic purposes

All archaeologists need to be aware of these rights and ensure they are respected or ensure that contracts include the necessary waiver of these rights.

"Fair Dealing" and Permitted Acts

There are a number of "fair dealing" and other provisions within the 1988 UK Copyright Act for individuals, libraries, and archives. Providing the use of copyright material falls within these provisions no permission from the copyright holder or payment of a royalty is required. Examples include:

- "Fair Dealing"- a single copy of a work for the purposes of research or private study, criticism or review

- Preservation copying by a library or archive

These provisions are important for both users and information providers accessing archaeological data in traditional formats. Museum curators should note that museums do not have the same institutional provisions for fair dealing as libraries or archives.

Contract Law

Licensing contracts employ contract rather than copyright law and allow information to be provided under stricter conditions than copyright law if necessary. As legal documents, advice on the precise wording of all standard terms and conditions in contracts/licences is essential. Effectively contracts may take two forms:

- an agreement [signed by all parties to the agreement] for goods or services in return for which a consideration is paid. These agreements are legally binding

- implied contracts eg shrink wrapped contracts included with CD ROMS or other software. As contract law only applies to terms you know about or should know about in advance such contracts are often regarded by lawyers as unenforceable. Even so they can be effective in persuading most people to follow their terms

Contract law may also be the only means for museums to protect their interests in out of copyright material by imposing conditions on its supply (if no publication rights are held) or for access to it.

Photography and Scanning by members of the public

In the past members of the public have occasionally been allowed to take their own photographs of museum material and requests to scan material are occasionally made. In most cases the museum will have no control over the private or commercial use of such photographs or scanned images which have been taken on their premises. Even if the user has agreed only to use the image for a specified purpose, the copyright may later be sold to a separate organisation or picture library who may not be bound by the agreement. Museums should therefore give careful consideration to this area, particularly for well known and 'commercial' objects.

Recent or Proposed Changes to Copyright Legislation

Publication Right

A new intellectual property right known as "Publication Right" has been introduced as a result of a Directive (EEC 1993) to harmonise copyright terms and related rights in member states by the European Commission.

A Statutory Instrument giving legal force in the UK to this Right came into force in December 1996. The Right applies to all works covered by copyright including literary works (eg manuscripts, computer software) or artistic works (eg photographs and maps).

A Publication right will come into existence in works where copyright existed at some point but has since expired, when the work is first "made available to the public" either by:

- issuing copies
- publication
- exhibition
- broadcast (eg TV, cable or online access)
- Making it "available for inspection" at an establishment open to the public

The publication right will not automatically be held by the owner or curator of the work but by the person/organisation who first makes the work available to the public. The Right will exist for 25 years from the end of the calendar year in which the work is first made available to the public. The Right can be assigned, or licensed in return for a royalty.

The Publication Right is potentially important to museums and other public repositories and may provide new intellectual property rights in some out of copyright and unpublished collections for archaeological organisations (or for others if it is overlooked).

EEC Directive on Copyright Term

The copyright term provisions of this directive (EEC 1993) was implemented in UK law from 1st January 1996 and has changed the term of copyright protection from the norm of "life plus 50 years" to "life plus 70 years". It extends by 20 years the copyright protection in works still in copyright and revives copyright in works where copyright has expired during the last 20 years. The duration of Crown copyright is unaffected by this change.

EEC Directive on Database Copyright

In March 1996 a new directive (EEC 1996) was announced by the EEC which will need to be enacted in UK law within 2 years.

The directive aims to give a degree of copyright protection to databases which might otherwise be excluded from copyright law. Current copyright law is designed to protect creativity and facts in themselves cannot be copyrighted: hence most databases have limited protection in law except where appropriate as compilations/literary works.

The directive defines a database as a collection of independent items accessed by electronic or other means. It confers rights for a period of 15 years to prevent certain actions eg extraction and re-utilisation of work. However others can take an "insubstantial" part. For protection under the directive to apply an organisation must demonstrate investment in a database in any of the following ways: verification of data, obtaining data, or its presentation.

If any of these processes are continuous then effectively the database will never be out of copyright as the protection rolls forward.

Electronic Media

It is important to recognise that there is no separate copyright for electronic media and that copyright in an electronic work is a sum of the parts, which are covered by existing categories of copyright material (photos, sound, etc) in analogue form. The EEC Directive on Database Copyright, when it is implemented in the UK, will therefore represent an important departure: the first time that an electronic medium is covered by separate legislation (although the term database will cover items in a collection accessed by electronic or other means).

Many of the difficulties in obtaining or drafting licences for electronic materials arise because of the particular challenges they represent in protecting the owner's rights. Electronic material can have very high resolution and be copied repeatedly with little or no degradation. Electronic images are therefore frequently only made available in low resolutions unsuitable for traditional publications, protected by encryption or watermarking, and/or are available with stringent licensing conditions.

The fact that electronic media are more easily manipulated and altered also means that maintaining the integrity of the information is a major issue. Most licences for electronic media even from archaeological projects need to consider the limits to alteration and manipulation permitted to prevent potential abuse. The authenticity and validation of electronic materials is also of far greater importance and increasingly problematic.

Another area of difficulty is that there is considerable uncertainty as to the legitimacy of fair dealing in electronic materials under current legislation. This is because a single copy of a work is permitted but the process of transmitting over a digital network or caching within a PC will always create additional, often transient, but potentially infringing copies. There is therefore potentially no "fair dealing" defence in using digital materials and you must acquire specific rights to make information available in digital formats.

The recent World Intellectual Property Organisation treaty negotiations have concluded and the treaty is open for signature by governments until December 1997. The treaty recognises that the principal of fair dealing should apply to electronic materials but there is considerable debate over its interpretation and it will be interesting to see how the governments who are signatories to the agreement implement the treaty (for further information see the WIPO web-site at http://www.wipo.int).

Conclusion

With many different issues facing museums it is easy for copyright issues to be looked upon as of little interest or of too great a complexity for professionals in the field to consider. However copyright is now central to the work of all museums and there are actions that all museum archaeologists can take to ensure that risks or benefits from copyright are properly managed:

- standardise documents for transfer of title and rights. Audit copyright in collections
- if copyright is not assigned, license the rights you need
- formalise permission letters and licences
- define (limit) rights in all permissions and licence
- use existing sources of advice and guidance. Seek legal advice on any specific problems you face
- consider copyright at the beginning of all projects not the end

Museum archaeologists must now always address copyright as part of any acquisition or in drawing up contracts, and consider copyright at the outset of projects. Although copyright can be daunting for individuals alone to consider, there are many organisations within the archaeological and museum communities or in related areas that have combined or can combine, to develop frameworks and licences for archaeological or museum use. Archaeologists can draw on experience in a wide range of institutions from museums (eg Museums Association 1997), or libraries (eg Oppenheim et al 1996) to photo archives (eg membership of BAPLA- The British Association of Picture Libraries and Agencies).

A good example of what is available is the guidance and model transfer of title and copyright, or copyright licences for archaeological archives developed by the Society of Museum Archaeologists on behalf of its members with funding from the Museums and Galleries Commission (Owen 1995, 14-19 and 61-67). Another is the common Rights Management Framework and licences being developed for digital collections held by the five Services (Archaeology, History, The Oxford Text Archive, Performing Arts, and Visual Arts) forming The Arts and Humanities Data Service, which has been established within the UK Higher Education sector (full details of this Framework and licences will be available from the AHDS web pages at http://ahds.ac.uk later in 1997).

References

EEC 1993 'Directive 93/98/EEC of 29 October 1993 harmonizing the term of protection of copyright and certain related rights' *Official Journal of the European Union* L290, 24.11.93, 93ff

EEC 1996 'Directive 96/9/EC of 11 March 1996 on the legal protection of databases' *Official Journal of the European Union* L77, 27.3.96, 20ff

HMSO 1988 *The Copyright, Designs and Patents Act* HMSO London

Museums Association 1997 *New Developments in Copyright* Museums Briefing 13, January 1997

Oppenheim, C., Phillips, C., and Wall, R A 1996 *The Aslib Guide to Copyright* Release 4

Owen, J (ed) 1995 *Towards An Accessible Archaeological Archive* Society of Museum Archaeologists

THE SURREY MUSEUMS ARCHAEOLOGY SURVEY

Hedley Swain, Museum of London Archaeology Service

This paper originated in the work I carried out in 1994 and 1995 for the Surrey Museums Archaeological Survey (Swain 1995; Swain 1996). In the form it was presented at the 1996 SMA conference it also drew upon the results of my research into archaeological archive transfer. However, as that survey has now been published (Swain 1997) I have edited down this contribution to concentrate on the Surrey work.

It is inevitable that when one area comes under scrutiny the impression is given that any criticism or praise are particular. This is not the case and I have no reason to believe that Surrey is atypical of the country as a whole where similar arrangements exist: there is good and less good to report. If Surrey museums are to be singled out it is to praise the initiative of setting up the collections surveys, one of which is reported on here.

Surrey, a county of 'contrasts'

Surrey inevitably suffers from its close proximity to London. Much of its population work in, or are tied economically to, the capital. Although in places very rural, much is built up with housing and the amenities associated with suburbia: shopping centres, golf courses, motorways. Its north and east are in effect outer suburbs of London. It has one major town, the historic city of Guildford and several small to medium sized market towns: Farnham, Dorking and others. Much of the west of the county is dominated by the army, its barracks and training grounds, centred around Camberley .

Archaeologically London has also had a profound effect. Much of Historic Surrey is now in Greater London: County Hall is actually in the London Borough of Kingston. Many of those who undertook field work in the county travelled out from London and returned afterwards, taking their findings with them. The old adage that archaeological distribution maps reflect railway stations and walking distances from them rather than actual archaeological patterns is probably particularly true of Surrey. Although there is a rich archaeological heritage (for a summary see Bird and Bird 1988) there are very few monuments that can be visited,

thus putting added responsibility on museums as the sole communicators of local history.

So for much of the county's population a 'sense of place' may be difficult to identify. Certainly it is difficult to think of Surrey in terms of an identifiable historic or geographic entity in the same way one can identify such areas as, for example, Wiltshire, Devon, even Kent and Sussex. Where there is local identity it tends to be focused on particular towns rather than the county as a whole.

This situation has not been helped by museum development and coverage. No county museum service exists or has ever existed so coverage is uneven, mixed and un-integrated. Museums tend to be supported by local district authorities, or, as in the majority of cases, by local voluntary societies aided by local authorities (Fig 1). The most common institution is a small town museum run by the local archaeology, historical or natural history society in a building donated, or made available rent free, by the district council. You might see this as a perfect partnership, or as a local authority providing a museum service on the cheap!

Although I would not decry the efforts of those involved, or demean the end result, museums run and staffed by part-time volunteers almost inevitably results in a lack of specialist curatorial and period knowledge, minimal funding for collections care, management and display and a piecemeal and isolated provision for the region as a whole. The exception is where a particular individual has built up a strong local knowledge. However, in such cases what happens when that individual dies or moves on? There are several cases of museums in Surrey with large, well ordered collections which are the legacy of a previous generation of active archaeologists and are now in the care of social historians or naturalists who have a minimal understanding of the material.

The exception to the general rule with museums in Surrey is Guildford Museum, which is large and well served by displays and professional staff. As a result, and by default, it has taken on many of the roles of a county museum including the acquisition of county wide material despite its district council funding. Guildford Museum also houses the collections and acts as a headquarters for the Surrey Archaeological Society, one of the largest and best endowed in the country thanks to the astute management of a major bequest. A number of other local authority museums are supported by professional staff and have achieved much in the way of display and educational resources from limited funding.

perience of dealing with large and complex collections management problems and supported by a broad theoretical understanding of museum archaeology.

The brief was to visit all museums and institutions in the county with archaeology collections (this turned out to be seventeen museums, one voluntary archaeological

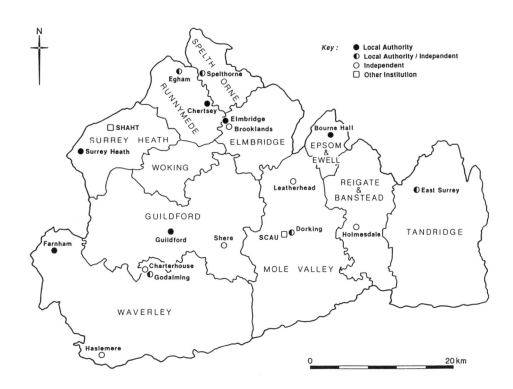

Fig 1 Museums with Archaeological Collections in Surrey

The Surrey Museums Archaeology Survey
Although with no county museum service some attempt at strategic county provision is attempted by two committees: the Surrey Museums Consultative Committee, made up of councillors, curators and others; and the Surrey Curators Group. Professional continuity is provided in the person of the Surrey Museums Development officer, a post funded from both county and district councils. As part of its work the SMCC is funding a series of collections surveys. The first was geology, the second archaeology, the third, which has just begun, costume.

The brief for the archaeology survey was issued in September 1994, tenders were sought and a contract of £10,000 offered. MoLAS applied, was interviewed and offered the contract. We qualified as a large team of museum artefact specialists and conservators with ex-

trust and the county archaeology section, illustrated on Fig 1); and prepare a report on each institution covering such areas as display, collections management, storage, education, conservation). Secondly a database was designed to hold a summary of all archaeology in museums: I will return to this shortly. Finally a strategic report was prepared summarising the nineteen individual reports and making recommendations for future needs (Swain 1995).

The practicalities of the survey were straightforward. Each visit was initially given one day and was undertaken by myself and a conservator. Basic *pro formas* were devised to ensure we recorded consistent information about displays, stores, etc. Basic environmental monitoring equipment was used. Some museums had to be revisited to complete work and in a few cases the second visit included a MoLAS finds specialist to help with the assessment of large assemblages of material. To avoid specialist visits to see individual objects a polaroid camera was used.

On a practical level the survey sought to obtain objective information in a number of areas so that recommendations could be made both for individual museums and museums in general. Also so that immediate and considered advice could be given to curators. The MGC Standard for archaeological collections was used as a benchmark in undertaking this work.

The areas covered in each report were:

• summary of collections
• provenance of collections
• collections management
• environmental management of collections on display and in store
• significance and potential of collections for: interpretation and education; academic research

Diplomacy played an important part of the survey. I was very conscious that we were from a large well funded and 'professional' organisation from outside the county. We were there to pass judgement, 'report back', criticise. Spending time to get to know curators was important, wherever possible we compared problems at the Museum of London with their own. We made a point of allowing curators to take the lead in identifying potential problems.

We found everyone was very friendly and in most cases fully accepted the need for archaeological advice. Our conservators were particularly welcome; often they could sort out a whole range of minor problems there and then and put curators minds at rest. The lack of conservation coverage was identified as a major problem. Voluntary staff may have a background interest in archaeology and be able to acquire basic knowledge about collections management, but conservation and collections care are another matter altogether. In some cases we found that serious conservation problems were imminent because basic rules of storage and packaging were not known.

The database, known as SMAD (Surrey Museums Archaeology Database) is potentially an important innovation. It coded all archaeology in Surrey museums by a number of fields: parish found, period, material type and form, and origin, a list of pre-set terms were used for this. The material was loaded onto a db4 database, not the most innovative software package but one that is widely used and understood. In theory material can

be sorted by any field: where is the Iron Age pottery in Surrey museums, what has been found in the parish of Weybridge? which museums is it in? The only weakness of the system is that the database does not correlate to museum accessions; time and practicality did not allow for this. So when you know, for example, that there are five Neolithic axes in Haslemere Museum you must ask the curator to find them using their own system. There is obviously the possibility of extending the system to allow for accession identification at a future date if it is deemed useful.

Nevertheless to the serious researcher or interested member of the public the database should save valuable time. Indeed it has already done so for the present national survey of late prehistoric ceramics. It should also have uses in planning future exhibitions within Surrey museums and could lead to sensible rationalisation of collections. We found many examples of material kept in museums well away from their find-spot and a few examples of excavation archives split between several museums. Ultimately use of the directory could liberate the potential research value of small museum collections. Instead of being seen as purely local collections they can be researched as part of the overall archaeological resource for the county along with the SMR and published sources. It is an interesting observation that we often found it very difficult to tie up older publication reports with archives in museums. The database should help researchers doing this in the future.

The state of museum archaeology in Surrey
Without dealing in particulars the survey has shown several things. Where no county museum service exists, provision will be very mixed. For example we found that some curators religiously kept the county SMR informed of finds while at another museum twenty miles down the road they had never heard of the SMR. The quality of display and the importance of archaeology is very much down to individual curators or groups when standards are not being imposed centrally. Museums run by professional, archaeology-trained staff inevitably are better equipped to deal with archaeology acquisition, display and interpretation. We should not be afraid to admit this as obvious. A number of museums in Surrey, both professionally and non-professionally staffed, have regionally important collections, imaginative displays and good collections management systems. Others are run by voluntary staff with no archaeological experience and no time to gain it. Often these museums do have archaeological collections and inevitably these are not cared for as well as professional museum archaeologists would wish.

Interestingly, we came across a number of curators with an archaeology first degree. However, most had lost interest in archaeology concentrating instead on social history and education, the two subjects most relevant to small local museums. As we started the survey museums were preparing for their VE Day exhibition. As we finished they were preparing for their William Morris centenary exhibition! Archaeology is 'perceived' as a difficult subject to display. As such few attempt anything adventurous. One display case with a Beaker, three flint axes and two corroding bronzes set off by a sprig of heather and some astro turf seems to be the norm: archaeology as table display! Some museums had given up on archaeology all together. At Farnham Museum, an area rich in Palaeolithic, Mesolithic and Roman sites, no archaeology is on permanent display (apart from two Palaeolithic axes stuck to the floor in the introductory gallery). Archaeology was banished to the stores in the recent re-design of the museum; visitor surveys showing that recent social history was more popular. It gives a new angle to the post-processual, post-modernist argument that your granny is as qualified to interpret Stonehenge as Richard Atkinson. In this case your granny probably is best qualified to interpret the material culture being displayed: she once owned it.

This is a situation that we, as archaeologists, should be concerned with. Throughout the country small local museums with archaeological collections try to cover a range of topics but almost inevitably concentrate on social history.

What is definitely the case is that the new system of field archaeology being contracted out and undertaken by non-local units has left many museums out of touch with what is going on in their area. Contact between museums and the rest of the archaeological community seemed minimal. When the local public want to know something about archaeology they will normally go to their local museum. It must be very frustrating when that local museum knows no more than them.

Conclusions

Our recommendations called for some form of county-wide archaeological expertise to be provided. We also called for similar conservation coverage and training in basic conservation care: for example good packaging and handling. Inevitably there is also a need for extra storage; and for storage with suitable environmental conditions. Too many Surrey museums have stores which are too small or not suitable for archaeology collections. We all know it to be the case that funding bodies and museum managers have not allocated the resources needed to store reserve collections properly, even though by doing so they create new expense in conservation for the future.

We recommended a county store to take excavation material and the overflow from existing museum collections. This and the other recommendations will cost money and at present it is unclear what will be achieved. Another recommendation, and perhaps more practical, is that the different museum and field archaeologists in Surrey start communicating better. An archaeology curators group has been set up and is at present working on a series of guidelines .

Surrey through its museum agencies should be warmly congratulated on commissioning the survey. For Surrey we now know the state of museum archaeology and have concrete proposals for the future. Funding may not be forthcoming to correct all identified problems but at the least the museum community has identified what needs to be done and can slowly work to make improvements. In the meantime those parts of the museum archaeology community in Surrey which are well served are now in a position to network.

Acknowledgements
I am grateful to Dana Goodburn-Brown and Kirsten Suenson-Taylor who undertook the conservation element of the projects and commented on the original text. Peter Hinton read and commented on this text. The map is by Susan Banks.

References
Bird, D and Bird, J (ed) 1987 *The Archaeology of Surrey to 1540*

Museum and Galleries Commission 1992 *Standards in the Museum care of Archaeological Collections*

Swain, H 1995 *Archaeology in Surrey Museums*

Swain, H 1996 The Surrey Museums Archaeological Collections Survey *Surrey Archaeological Society Bulletin* September 1996, 304, 7

Swain, H 1997 Archaeological Archive Transfer: Theory and Practice *The Museum Archaeologist* 22

PROBLEMS AND PRACTICALITIES IN ARCHIVE-BASED RESEARCH

Joanna Brück, Department of Archaeology, Cambridge University

The last few years have seen a considerable increase in awareness of the problems surrounding the collation and management of archaeological archives. While it is clear that there are still major issues to be resolved, discussion generated by organisations such as the SMA, IFA and RCHME and initiatives such as the publication of the SMA guidelines (1995) constitute an important step towards enabling a fuller use of the archival resource. Such reviews have isolated three main areas of concern:

- Access: why is access to archaeological archives important, and for whom should it be available?
- Quality and condition: how easy is it to retrieve information from archaeological archives?
- Storage: is it necessary to conserve all elements of an archive and if so, how can long-term storage demands be met?

In this short paper, I shall consider the role of excavation archives in archaeological research. The concerns that I shall discuss relate largely to access, quality and condition. They stem from my own experience of using archaeological archives for PhD research on Bronze Age settlements in southern England. The examination and interpretation of unpublished archival data has formed an important component of my research. However, I have found that in many cases the full potential of archives cannot be realised, while in others the condition of archives is too poor to enable detailed re-evaluation of the sites in question. While these problems are widely recognised, their implications are only beginning to be discussed. In this paper, then, I shall focus on the practicalities of archive use. I shall attempt to pinpoint the sources of the problems that I have experienced and shall discuss to what extent these may be resolved through adherence to guidelines such as those published by the SMA (1995). The implications of such problems with respect to archive management will also briefly be considered.

Access: Some general concerns

The issue of access is one that has been consistently highlighted within recent discussions of archaeological archives. This concern must be contextualised within broader debates that have arisen within museums and the heritage industry generally, namely the role of museums within an ever diversifying social framework and, perhaps more relevant here, the issue of responsibility towards a public who in many cases provide a large proportion of museum funding. The question 'whose museum?' must be accompanied by the question 'whose archive?'. That museums are the appropriate repositories for archival material has long been accepted, but the resources in terms of time and money that are put into archive management and conservation are not matched as yet by the degree to which archives are used by either the public or the academic community. It seems self-evident that one of the most important roles of museums is to safeguard the people's heritage *for* the people, yet too often this is transformed into saving the people's heritage *from* the people. The irony in this situation is all too clear. In many of the museums I have visited as a researcher, I was the only person looking at material in the reserve collection over the period of a week-long or even a fortnight-long stay.

It is obviously not the case that access is being actively denied: in my own experience, museum staff have been consistently positive and facilitating. In fact, the problem lies at a much more subtle level. The myth of archive repositories as dusty places of storage and safe-keeping is deeply ingrained in the public imagination. The difficulty of obtaining information on the whereabouts and contents of particular archives, and the lack of facilities for those wishing to use them at most museums, suggests that this concept may also be shared by many museum professionals. What is required is a more active image of archives as resources for education, research and recreation. This means breaking down the barriers between museum galleries and behind the scenes, between professionals, amateurs and visitors. This may be a difficult task, but it is one that is already being undertaken at museums across Britain. Such a process will ultimately legitimate the existence of museums and enhance their relevance to the public in a way that is bound to be beneficial to museums in the long term. At a national level, the development of the National Monuments Record is an important primary step. At a regional and local level, disseminating information to the public and encouraging fuller and more varied public use of archives will be a central part of the process. No doubt, developments in information technology will have a major impact over the next ten to twenty years. Already, a number of museums can be accessed on the World Wide Web; their Web pages provide pictures and information on some of the finds in their collections. Clearly, this kind of access has the potential to transform completely the nature of the interface between museums, researchers and the public.

Archives and archaeological research

These commonplace observations raise the question of what is an archive actually for? From the viewpoint of an academic researcher, the main role of an archive is to allow the re-interpretation of archaeological sites. The development of archaeology as a discipline is predicated on our ability to bring new questions, techniques, and theoretical frameworks to bear on data that have already formed the basis for a particular interpretation of the past. Without the existence of an archive, only those questions that the excavator thought interesting can ever be considered. Perhaps more fundamentally, recent debates in archaeology have highlighted the importance of being able to write alternative accounts of history and prehistory: the plural voices of post-modernist society have come to claim their versions of the past. In other words, archives are central to the continued creation, evaluation and contestation of knowledge.

Furthermore, an archaeological archive forms a repository for a whole range of detailed information that would prove too costly to publish fully. With the increase in developer-funded archaeology, more and more excavations are taking place, each of which adds to the proliferation of archaeological data in existence. The need for publication is widely recognised, yet the cost of doing so is frequently prohibitive. As early as 1975, the Frere report (DoE 1975) recognised the potential role of a well-organised and accessible archive in alleviating this problem. As such, the curation of archaeological archives is of particular importance. Yet, the flip side of this coin is the cost to museums of storing, maintaining and conserving archives in perpetuity. If a sustainable solution cannot be achieved, then the whole archaeological enterprise is called into question.

While it is clear that archives are central to archaeological research, can the needs of researchers really legitimate the curation of archives? As Nick Merriman pointed out at the conference, the total number of academic researchers utilising museum archives is extremely small. He argued that catering to the requirements of visiting researchers is therefore of necessity a low priority for any museum. Merriman's observations highlight the real need to clarify the role of archaeological archives, both in terms of the academic and public domains, and to encourage the use of archives in a much wider range of non-research and public-oriented activities. While the archival resource is underused, as seems to be currently the case, it will be extremely hard to argue for the curation of all archaeological archives in perpetuity, and even more difficult to obtain funding for storage facilities.

At the same time, however, the value of academic research should not be underestimated, even if the number of researchers using museum collections seems all too small at present. Ultimately, the interpretations presented to the public by museum professionals are based on such work. Thus, research access to museum collections indirectly benefits both museums and the public. Indeed, one might argue that without such ongoing research it would be impossible for museums to present the kinds of exhibitions frequently argued to be most appropriate within the context of contemporary multicultural society, that is, reflexive narratives in which alternative interpretations of the past are evaluated. There are obvious ways in which museums could benefit more fully from work undertaken by visiting researchers, for example by requesting copies of any papers written using material from their collections. At present, it is not clear whether the small number of researchers visiting museum collections is the result of a real lack of interest in re-interpreting primary data or whether this relates more closely to perceived difficulties in accessing and using archives (see below). It certainly seems likely that such initiatives as the development of the NMR will encourage increased academic use of the archival resource in future.

Access: practical issues

Let us return to the practicalities of using archives for research purposes. Issues of access are of particular importance here. Museum staff are fully aware of their obligation to provide access to researchers and have been helpful and accommodating throughout my PhD research. Where finds and documentary archives remain in the hands of the excavator, however, this may be more difficult. Excavation archives frequently take several decades to make their way to the museum where they are to be deposited and in the interim they usually cannot be viewed. Neil Beagrie (1996) has quantified this tendency: of the 13,000 excavations recorded by the

National Monuments Record for the period 1940-1980, only 37% had final reports published by 1991. Of these, 72% of finds archives had been deposited in the appropriate museums but only 51% of documentary archives. The situation for unpublished sites can hardly be any better and this gives us some idea of the number of archaeological archives to which access may be difficult if not impossible. The issue is complicated by the fact that such archives have not yet reached the public domain. Legal ownership of the finds resides with the landowner and that of the documentary archive with the excavator.

Such problems of access are particularly acute for sites excavated before the advent of archaeological units. Until the 1970s, an excavator's name was frequently made on the basis of a single site, thereby encouraging a proprietorial relationship between site and director. Subsequent re-interpretation of an archive might therefore be thought to endanger the excavator's credibility. The maintenance of such a proprietorial relationship into the present frequently hinders the re-evaluation and contestation of archaeological knowledge because researchers are denied access to the material in question. In the case of more recent excavations by archaeological units, I have found that the question of access tends to be less of an issue; units seem more willing to grant access to their excavation archives insofar as they can without compromising customer confidentiality. This perhaps relates to the larger turnover of sites and the frequent sharing of responsibility among supervisors, site directors, managers and specialists.

Now, the reader may quite reasonably argue that such problems lie outside the domain of the museum. On the other hand, the SMA guidelines (1995) explicitly state that the relevant archaeological repository must play a central role in negotiating how and when archives are to be transferred from excavator to museum, not least because of the considerable time and resources that the museum will need to budget for this process. The common perception of excavator as donor and museum as receiver is part of the problem. Given the responsibility and cost of storing an archive in perpetuity, the process is more appropriately seen as a two-way transaction; a joint effort to conserve the public heritage with give and take on either side. This means that the museum in question is in a good position to negotiate to its advantage and to ensure that the transfer of archives to the public domain occurs within a reasonable period of time after the end of an excavation. The SMA guidelines (1995) encourage collaboration between archive repositories and field archaeologists before the inception of field projects and recommend that archives should be deposited in the appropriate museum within a year of the end of fieldwork. No doubt, such dialogue between museum staff and excavator will help to secure rapid access to a much greater percentage of future excavations. Clearly, however, the backlog of sites dug many years ago still presents a problem. Until this is resolved the research potential generated by many excellent and possibly illuminating excavations is severely limited.

Once an excavation archive has been transferred to the relevant repository, such problems abate. However, access can still remain a problem, albeit at a different level. Where archives are poorly organised or documented (see below), location and retrieval of information may be difficult. The physical layout of museum storage facilities does not always help. For example, different parts of an archive may be stored in different places. Finds and paper archives are often stored separately and it may be impossible to view both together. At a very basic level, visiting researchers often find themselves working in a dusty basement or cold outside store, with little work space and poor lighting. Storage systems do not always provide easy access: on many an occasion, I have found myself perched on a rickety ladder trying to remove a heavy box from a high shelf. Again, we need to ask ourselves what are archives for? Is it our sole aim to ensure their preservation or are they also resources for use to which access should be actively encouraged? Recent debates within the museum profession have repeatedly stressed the latter. Storage facilities and work areas for visitors need to reflect and enable this aim. At present, however, the possibility of ameliorating the situation seems remote, not only because of a lack of resources but also because of contradictions built into current working practices. Because archives are underused, the provision of good work-areas for visitors has become a very low priority. However, it may be precisely because so many archives are user-unfriendly that neither researchers nor the public see the desirability of exploring their potential. Enhancing and promoting access to archives will not only legitimate their existence but may be one way of convincing government bodies that the archival resource should be properly funded.

Quality: Completeness

Once access has been granted, the researcher must assess the quality of the archive and its potential for his or her research aims. A first issue to consider is the completeness of the archive. Very many of the archives that I have examined are missing important elements and what appear, on the basis of their publications, to be promising sites may therefore turn out to be quite disappointing. For example, as late as the 1960s and

70s, the notes and plans produced during an excavation were not routinely deposited in the museum along with the finds. The view of many excavators at the time was that once the relevant information had been published, there would be nothing further to be gained by keeping the paper records. Obviously, as research aims and methodologies change, this becomes a problem. Although it is now standard practice to keep paper archives, this does underline the argument for the preservation of all material relating to an excavation; although we might not think it useful now, it may well be so in the future. Obviously, this approach is at odds with the spatial and financial resources of many museums. Once again, the disparity between aims and resources becomes a pivotal issue.

The completeness of an archive may also be affected by the timespan between excavation and transfer to the repository. Where the delay is a long one, it is often the case that components have gone missing over the years, so that the archive is only partial when it is finally transferred to the museum. For example, while examining the archive from one well-known site, I found it to be missing almost all of the plans and sections. Other problems arise when the different parts of an excavation archive still reside with a variety of specialists, even when the main body of the archive has reached the museum.

Organisation

When it came to collecting data from excavation archives, my own research was primarily concerned to record information on the context of individual finds. Surprisingly, this very basic kind of data was frequently impossible to obtain, even where the publication of a site had suggested that such information *was* recorded during excavation. In part, this problem relates again to the state of completeness of the archive. Equally important, however, is the organisation of the archive. Many archives have been very carelessly compiled, to such an extent that they may be all but unusable. Finds may not be labelled and the boxes in which they are stored may provide no clue as to context. There may be information on context for some of the finds but not for others. Different parts of the archive may provide quite contradictory information. Artefacts may have been renumbered at some stage but there may be no record of the relationship between old and new numbering systems. More practical difficulties arise when an archive is boxed in an awkward manner. To give a brief example, I was at one point working on a small assemblage of Bronze Age pottery from a multi-period site. Unfortunately this was distributed throughout a series of large

boxes full of Iron Age, Roman and Anglo-Saxon ceramics. Undoubtedly, much time is lost by both visiting researchers and museum staff in attempting to use poorly organised archives. Suffice it to say that the problem lies not only in obtaining the information from such archives, but in obtaining the *correct* information. All told, it can be a very frustrating experience.

Solving these problems

Now, these problems are well recognised. We all know that in theory a usable and accessible excavation archive will be complete, well-organised, catalogued, cross-referenced and boxed in a sensible way. The recommendations made by the SMA (1995) will no doubt go a long way towards ameliorating this situation. These highlight the need for field archaeologists and museum staff to work together from the very outset of a project and for the curator to monitor all stages of archive collation prior to transferral to the final repository. They advise that an agreement between both parties should be drawn up: this should follow the museum's archive preparation standards and must detail the responsibilities of all those involved. The long-term curatorial requirements of an archive must be taken into account during the process of archive preparation and compatible documentation systems should be used when creating the archive so that it will integrate smoothly into the existing museum system. In other words, archive repositories must produce clear professional criteria outlining what is acceptable practice and who is responsible for each stage of the process. Standards for such practicalities as the assignment of archive repository accession numbers, the carrying out of archive reviews at various different stages of the process, the format and content of the archive and the logistics of transfer must be drawn up. In summary, then, the SMA guidelines emphasise that the excavator has an obligation to provide museums with a complete and usable archive and that it is the curator's responsibility to facilitate and assist in this process.

Thus, the prospect for future archives looks more promising. But what of those that already exist? Many of the short-comings of these can never be solved: there is no way of retrieving missing site notebooks, for example. On the other hand, although the time and resources required of museum staff are bound to be considerable, organising and cataloguing older archives is a task that must be undertaken in order to assess and enhance their accessibility and usefulness. If it cannot be demonstrated that such archives are a usable resource, it will be difficult to legitimate the outlay of funds required to meet their long-term storage needs. No doubt the development of computerised documentation systems will go a long way towards resolving this problem and it may be fruitful to integrate projects such as the re-ordering of certain archives into long-term documentation aims. From a visiting researcher's point of view, the ideal situation would be for each museum's documentation system to hold information on the contents, state, completeness and detail of all excavation archives in the repository's collection. At present, it is rarely possible to find out whether an excavation archive can meet one's needs without travelling to the museum in question and examining the material in person.

Conclusion

To sum up, then, the potential usefulness of many of the archives currently housed in museums seems to be seriously restricted. No doubt, the drawing up of common guidelines for archive preparation and maintenance and the encouragement of good communication between excavators and curators will considerably improve standards in archaeological archiving. This is only part of the problem, however. The perennial lack of time and resources is clearly a major issue, but this cannot be used as an excuse. More fundamental, I would argue, is the series of contradictions that lies deeply embedded in current attitudes towards archives. If we cannot prove archives to be a useful and valuable resource, it will be increasingly difficult to legitimate the outlay of funds required to store and maintain them in perpetuity. On the other hand, it will be impossible to achieve this aim while the prevailing conception of archives as passive storehouses, interesting only to the most dusty academics, remains widespread. Clearly, a much more positive and proactive attitude to archives must be espoused before their accessibility and user-friendliness will be substantially improved. As the archaeological and museum communities are acutely aware, it is fast becoming impossible to deal with the ever-increasing quantities of data generated by developer-funded archaeology. Unless financial resources can be greatly enhanced, a serious crisis will be precipitated and the whole archaeological enterprise will be called into question: if we cannot store all of this newly-generated data, why bother excavating it in the first place? I must admit, here, to playing devil's advocate, but I hope this underlines the real need to reassess the role of the archival resource. An immediate and central aim must be to facilitate and encourage the use of archives by both the public and visiting researchers. In doing so, archaeologists and museum professionals will not only prove themselves fully accountable as guardians of the people's heritage, but they will also be able to present a much more convincing argument for the improvement of public funding for long-term archive curation.

References

Beagrie, N 1996 Museum collections, national archaeological indexes and research: information resources, access and potential *The Museum Archaeologist* 21, 28-34

Department of the Environment 1975 *Principles of publication in rescue archaeology: report by a working party of the Ancient Monuments Board for England, Committee for Rescue Archaeology* DoE

Society of Museum Archaeologists 1995 *Towards an accessible archaeological archive. The transfer of archaeological archives to museums: guidelines for use in England, Northern Ireland, Scotland and Wales* SMA

MUSEUMS IN THE LANDSCAPE: BRIDGING THE GAP OR WIDENING THE GULFS?

M. Hall, Perth Museum and Art Gallery

The 1996 Annual Conference built steadily and surely over its two days to leave in the mind a cumulative effect of probing deep into the profession to ask purposefully what it is we do and for whom. Two underlying threads (and threats) come repeatedly to the fore. Firstly the need for much greater communications between all branches of the archaeological community (and beyond). There seems little point in criticizing urban archaeological databases for something they were not set up to do but their potential to educate more widely should now begin to be exploited to the full. Yes, one can regret the narrow thinking that never took on board their wide potential from the start. For it is the same narrow thinking that fails to see the essential connectedness of the whole archaeological process which begins with people living in the past and ends with our custodianship of that inheritance, to be handed to future generations. It is in its present guise that we split up the process and force it into often opposing corners. This was evident to a degree at Conference. Researchers or rather specialist researchers (but meaning detailed academic researchers) seemed to be tagged as readily expendable: somehow what they do (or would wish to do) is only relevant to them. This does seem to forget the wider ethos of archaeology where all work, or should, to the benefit and the understanding of society as a whole. If such research does not contribute to this fundamental ethos then even those university museums whose principle public is researchers would rightly be in a position to question (or have questioned) the devotion of resources to this pursuit. Clearly, though, it is right to point out that the use of the archaeological archive by researchers needs to be balanced with other users. Communication between all parties concerned should enable more selective, rational and accessible archives: it is not the sole, isolated responsibility of museum archaeologists to ensure this.

Secondly we have the return of the perennial favourite, lack of resources. Nothing new I know but it does seem that in the last two years or so larger political events have pushed many local authorities (and national museums) well beyond the scope of natural wastage and efficiency savings. The cuts, and those impending, are increasingly fatal. The Lottery seems to be largely a shoring-up exercise which once more allows the government to avoid bigger responsibilities. This problem was little touched upon (but ever present) perhaps because we are all too aware of how all-encompassing it is and how little can seemingly be done.

One final point, as usual for SMA Conference, just as the final debate was getting going it was cut off by the timetable. Should we finish earlier to allow more time?

Oh, and a group of archaeologists is surely an assemblage (and if not, perhaps a 'spoil' or a 'pint').